For those who love the sea, in all its depth and mystery.

Mermaid Dreams- An Art Collection by Selina Fenech
First Published October 2012
Published by Fairies and Fantasy PTY LTD
ISBN: 978-0-9871511-8-6

www.selinafenech.com

Mermaid Dreams

AN ART COLLECTION BY SELINA FENECH

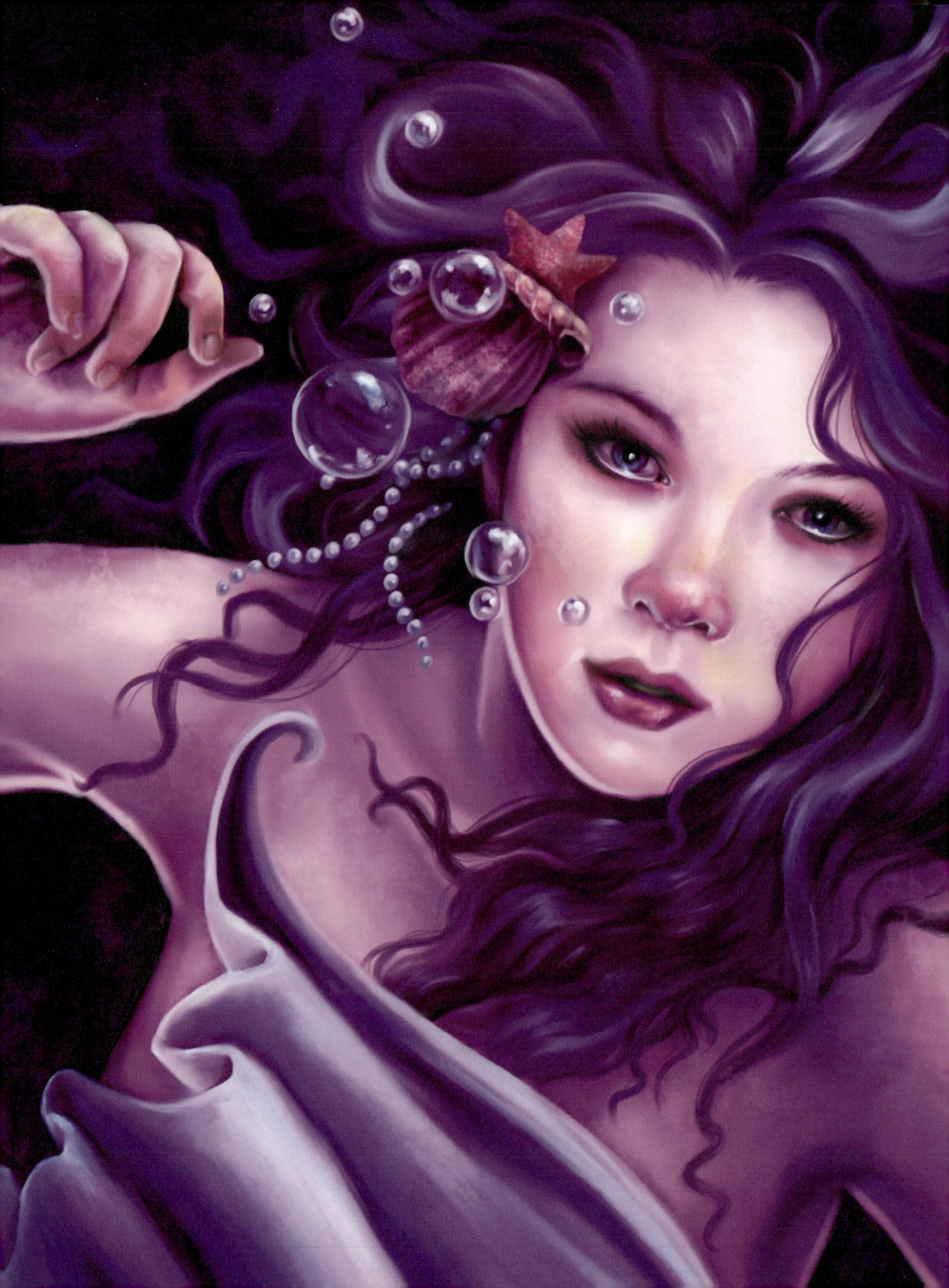

MERMAID DREAMS

AN ART COLLECTION BY SELINA FENECH

Mermaids are possibly Selina Fenech's favourite fantasy being, but also the one she finds the most challenging to portray. There is something about mermaids that is more sensual, wild, wise, and primal than their terrestrial counterparts, such as fairies. Mermaids are a part of many folklores and mythologies, often as predators, luring men to their watery graves. For Selina, mermaids are not so much intentionally cruel, as dangerously curious. They are beings of great beauty and strength and will do as they wish.

This collection showcases Selina's exploration of mermaids. Many of the images in this book were created for the Mermaid Oracle Deck for Blue Angel Publishing.

Left: "Indigo"
Digital (Photoshop and Wacom tablet), 2012

A Mermaid's Lament

Digital (Photoshop and Wacom tablet), 2012

A reworking of an older image, this mermaid rests at the shoreline with a look of longing. It was Selina's goal with this artwork to create a moving expression on the mermaid's face.

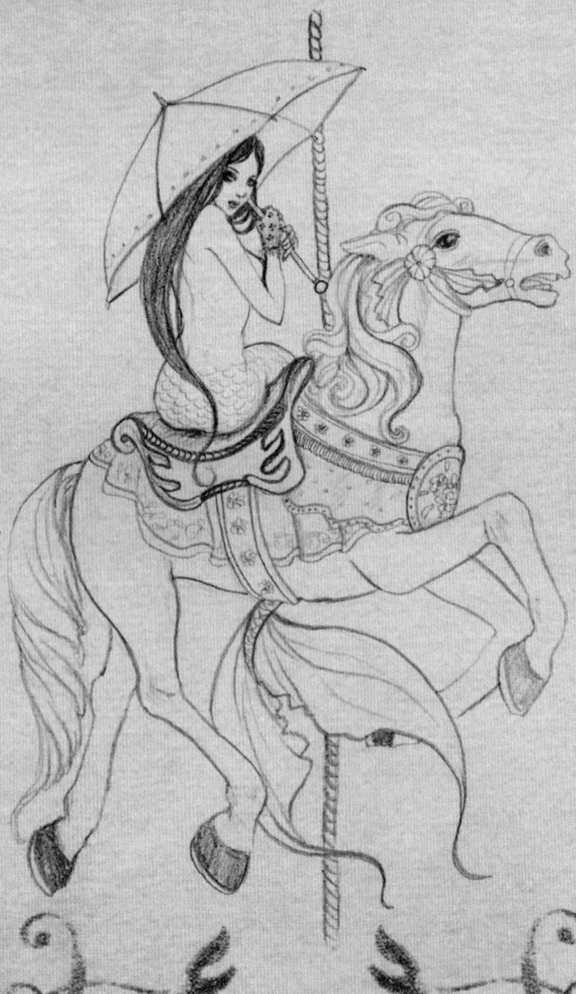

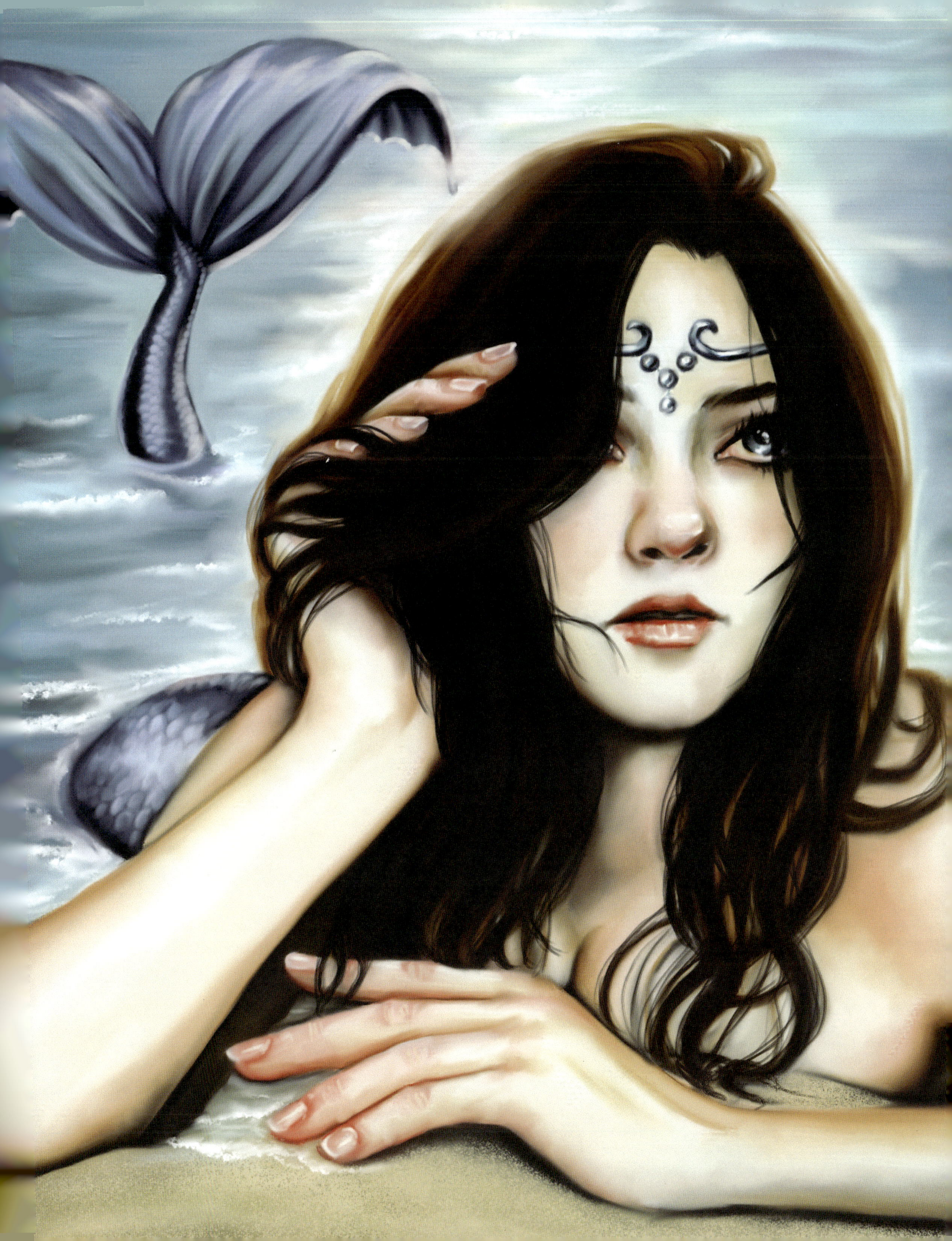

Wave of Power

Digital (Photoshop and Wacom tablet), 2012

A reworking of an older image (Lure), Selina wanted to create a sense of movement and power in the splash of the wave behind this mermaid. The mermaid is also freckled, both as a mirroring of the water spray texture, and because Selina thinks freckles are beautiful.

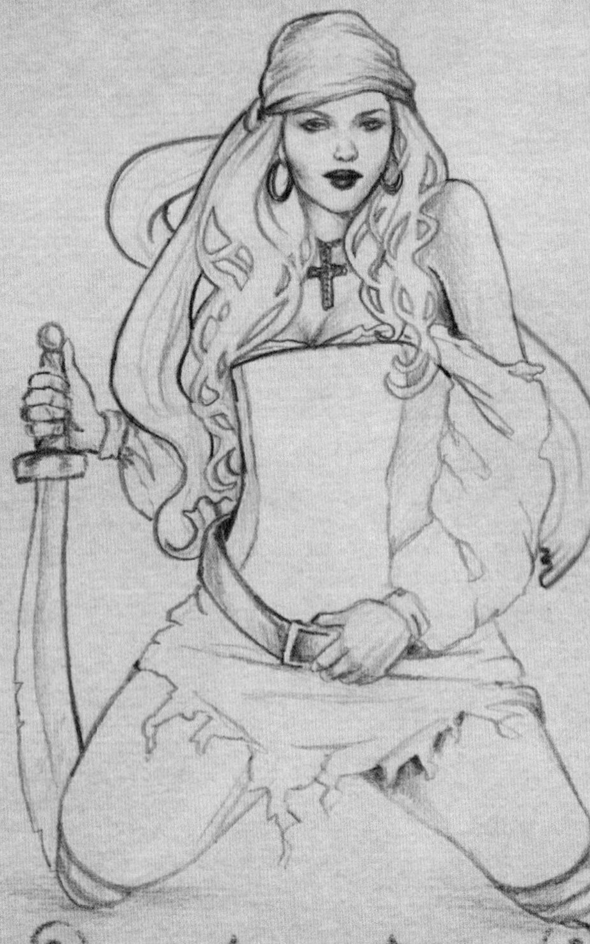

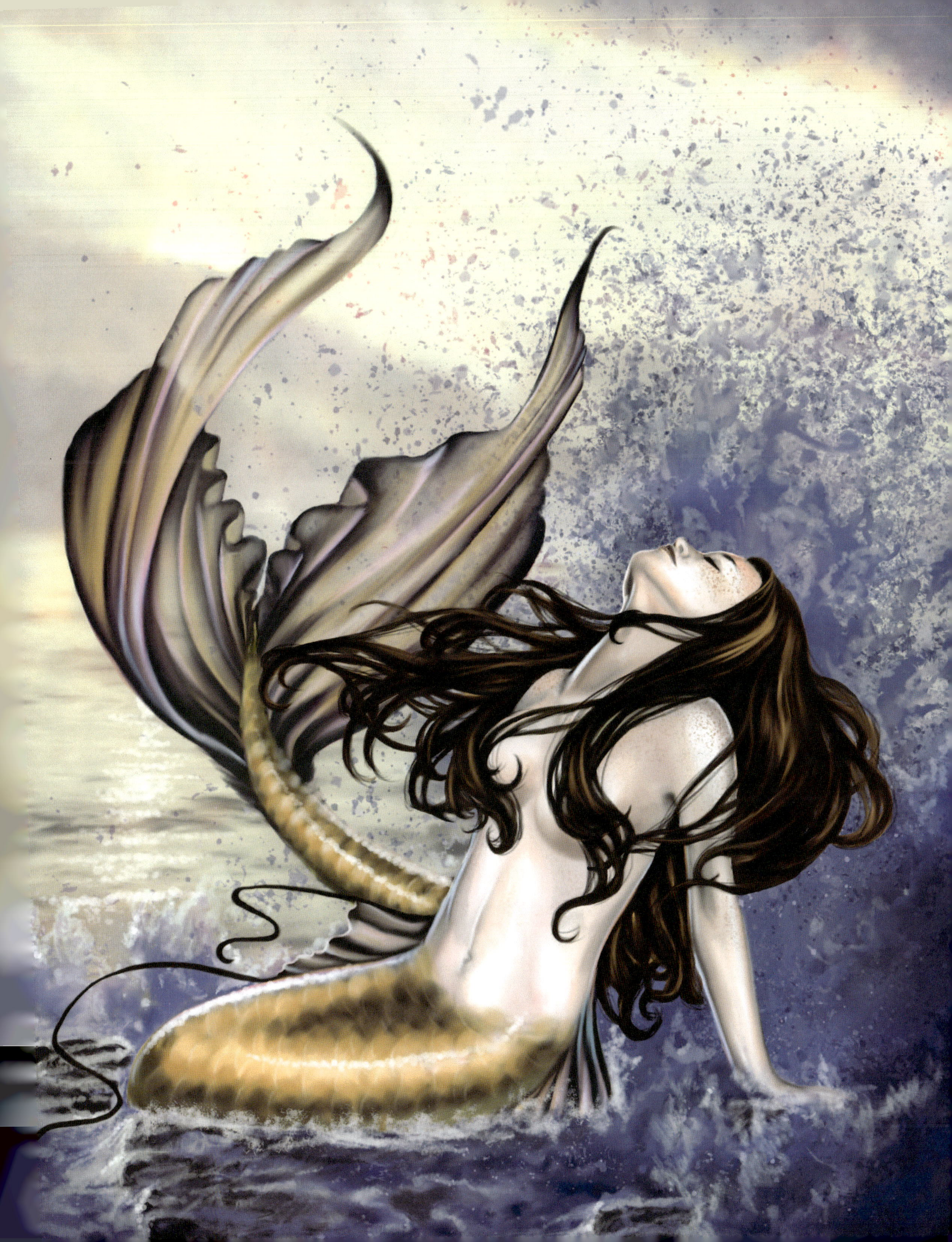

Shell Princess

Digital (Photoshop and Wacom tablet), 2012

A reworking of an older image (Sirena). A sense of depth of focus was used in this artwork by blurring the focus on the background so only the mermaid's face is in sharp focus, much like a photo with shallow depth of focus. Selina enjoyed creating the mermaids clothing and jewelry design with different shells.

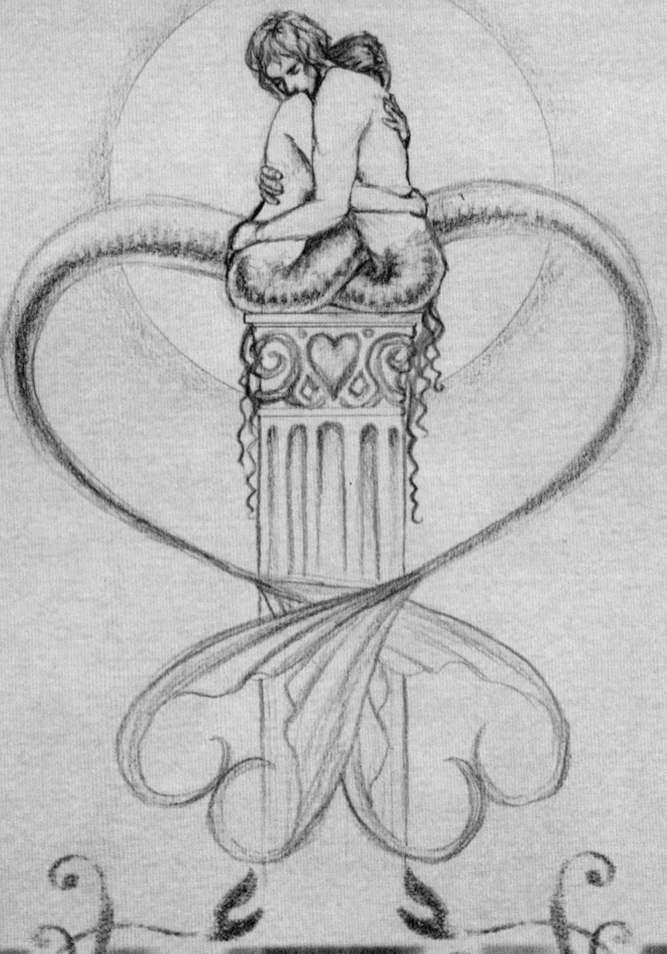

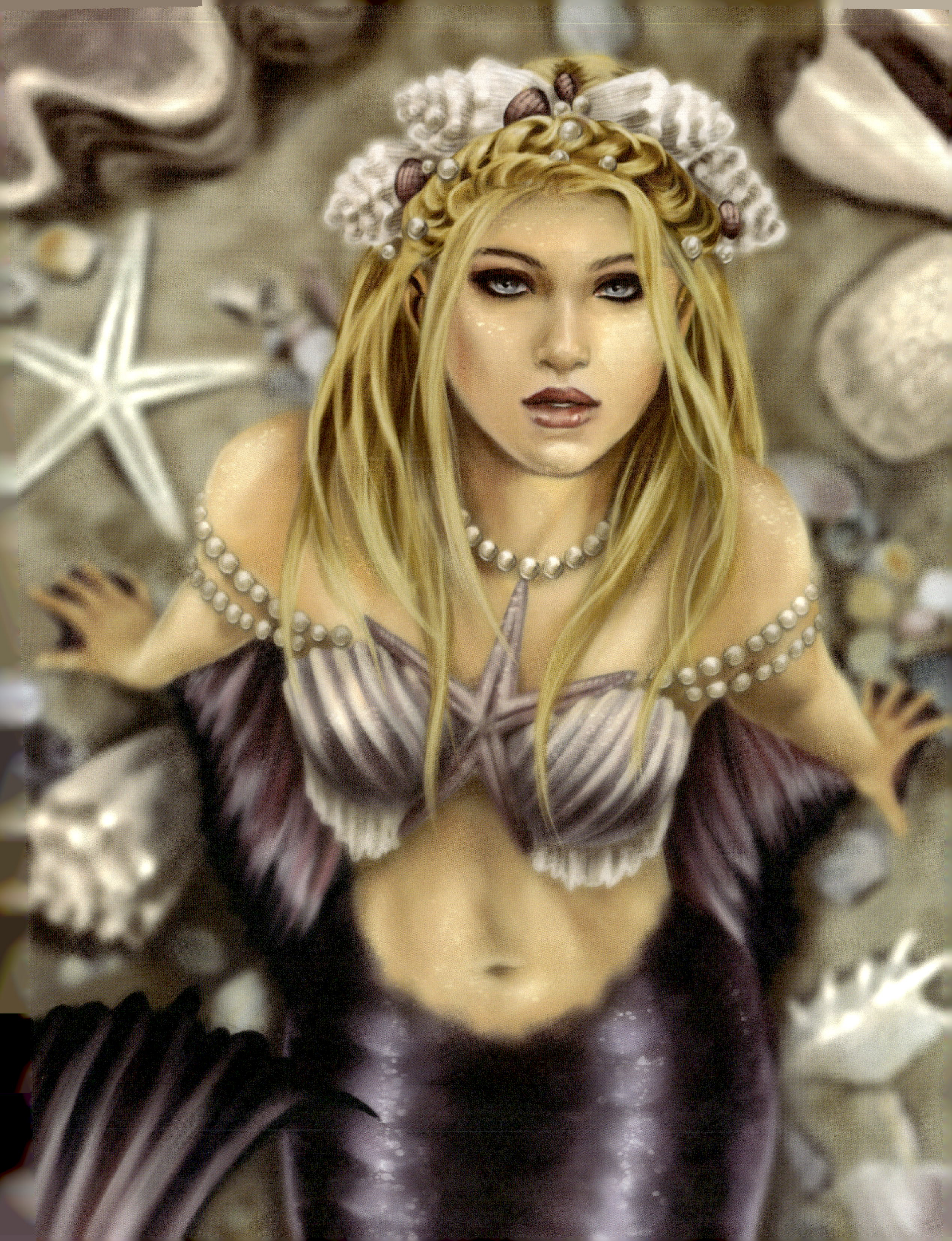

A Pirate's Life for Me

Acrylics on watercolour paper, 2007

This image was the result of a young girl asking Selina why her mermaids were naked. Selina's reply was "because their clothes would get wet", but the real reason was moreso that Selina doesn't see mermaids as the kind of creatures to spend their time making clothing. She believes mermaids would simply wear found objects that they consider beautiful, which is where the idea for this artwork came from. A mermaid who found a pirate's flag, and decided it would make fine clothing, indeed.

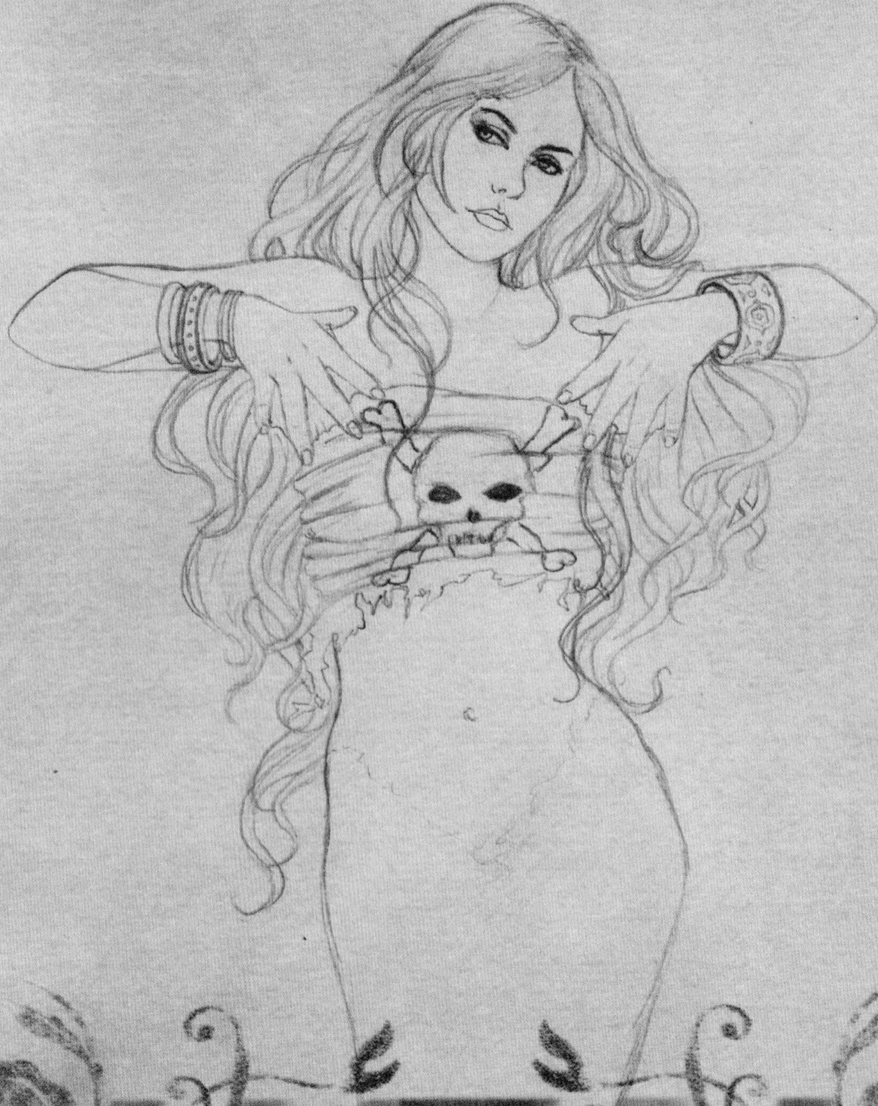

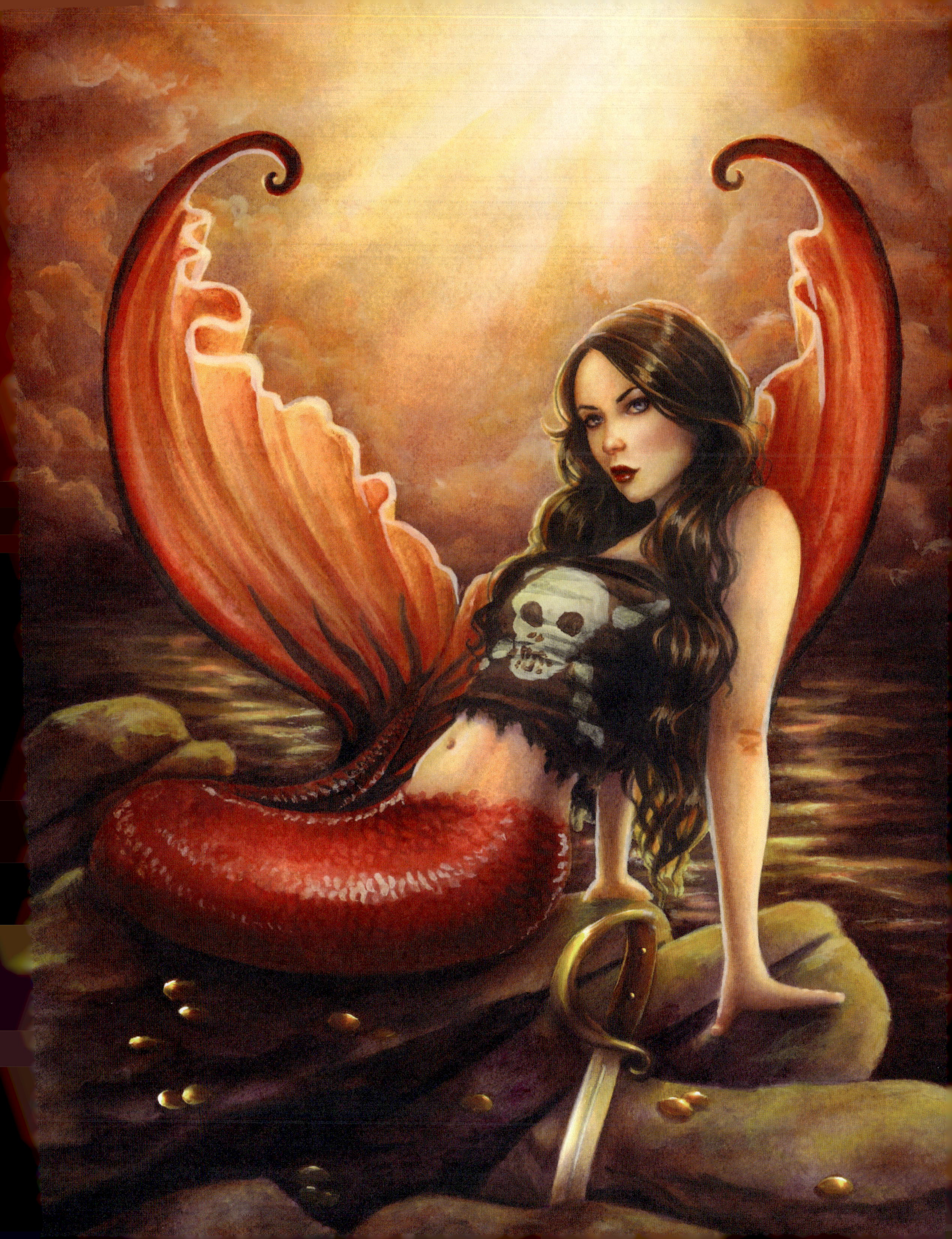

Pearl Princess

Digital (Photoshop and Wacom tablet), 2012

An updated version of the original "Pearl Princess", both artworks are very similar, and were painted by Selina with the goal of creating a very white, pearly image.

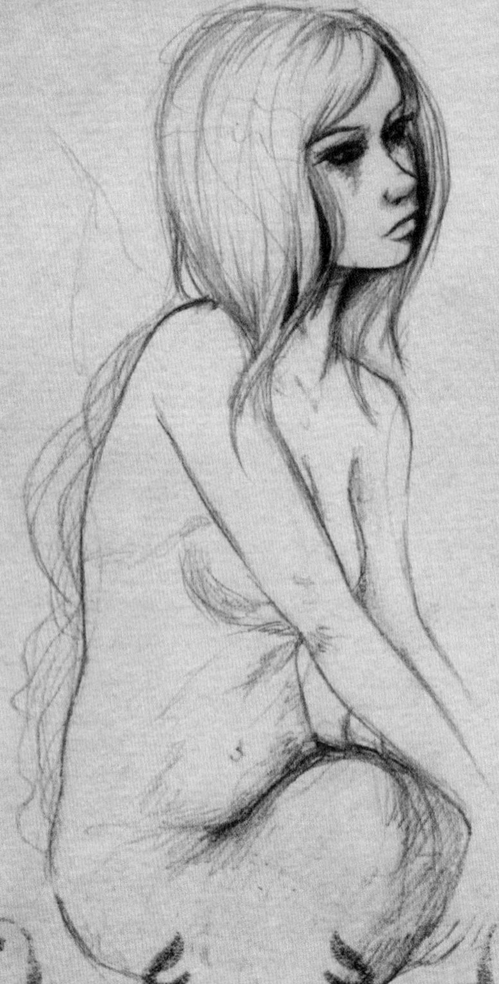

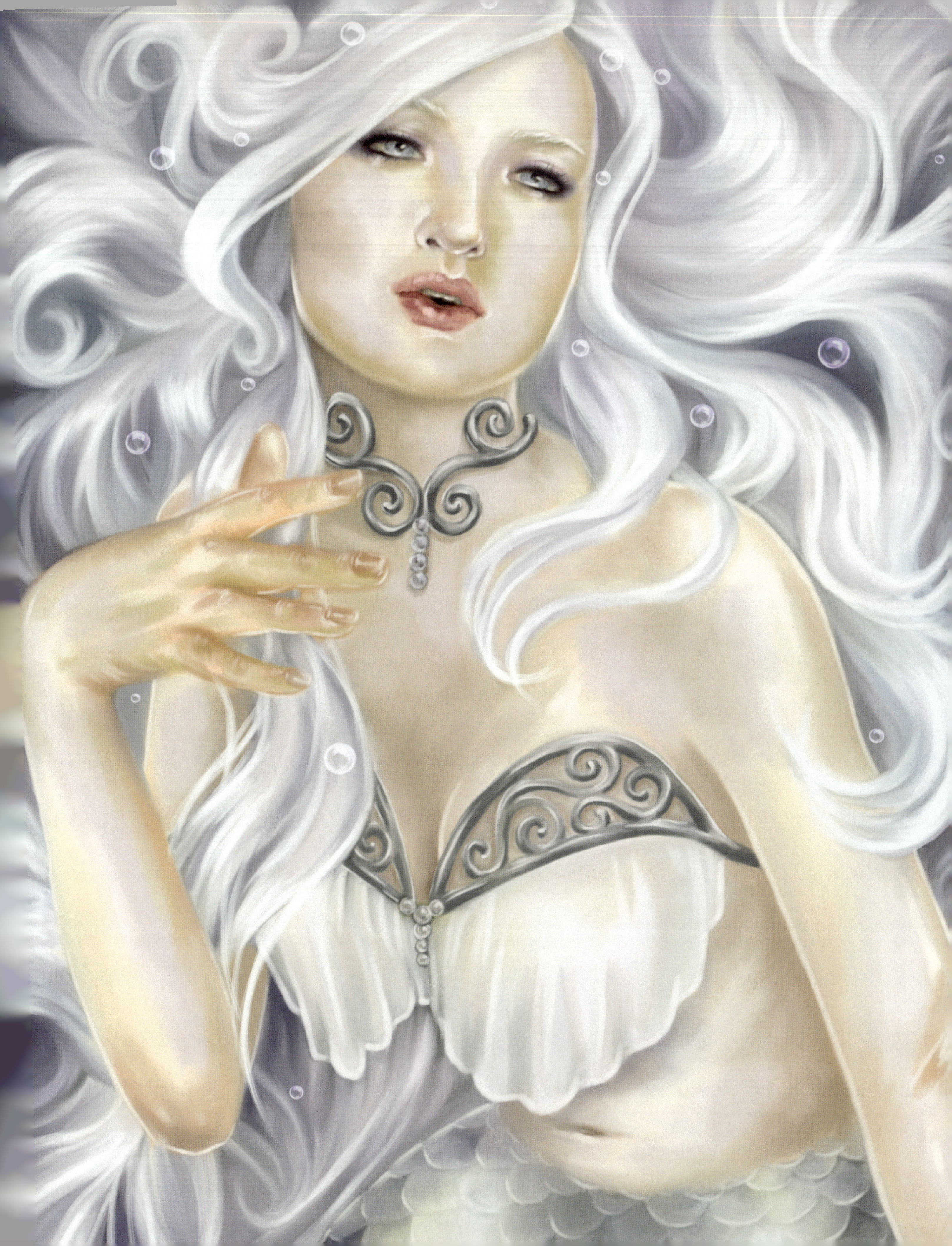

Underwater Secrets

Watercolour, acrylic and ink on watercolour paper, 2010

The mermaid in this artwork was inspired by a dream, in which Selina saw this mermaid with red hair floating about, putting her finger to her lips like she had a secret. The contradiction of the wing design tattooed on a creature of the sea adds further mystery.

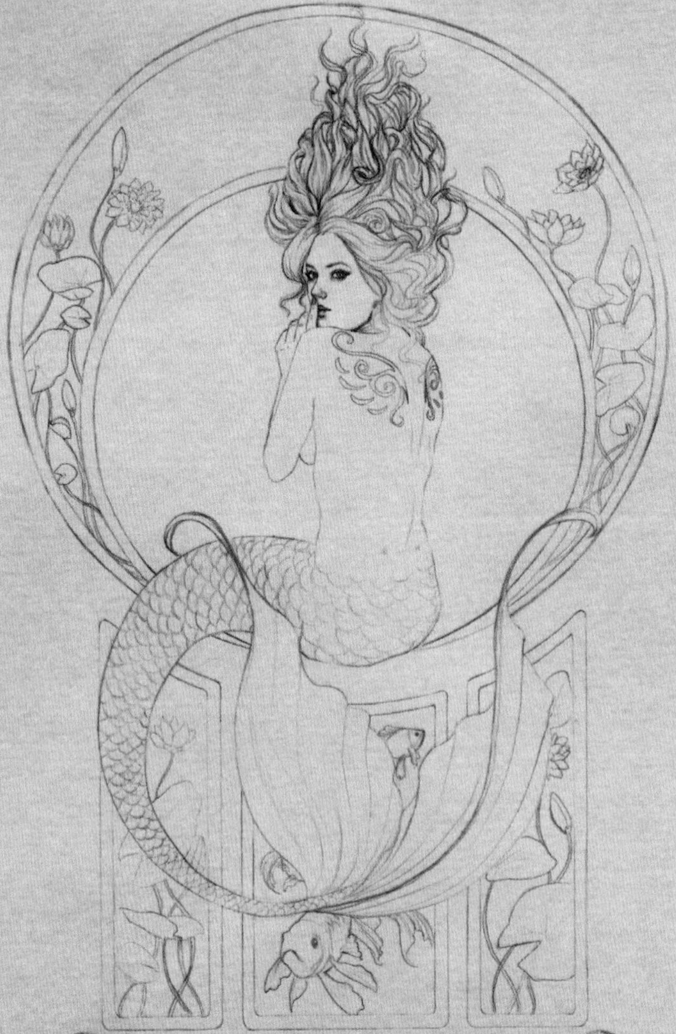

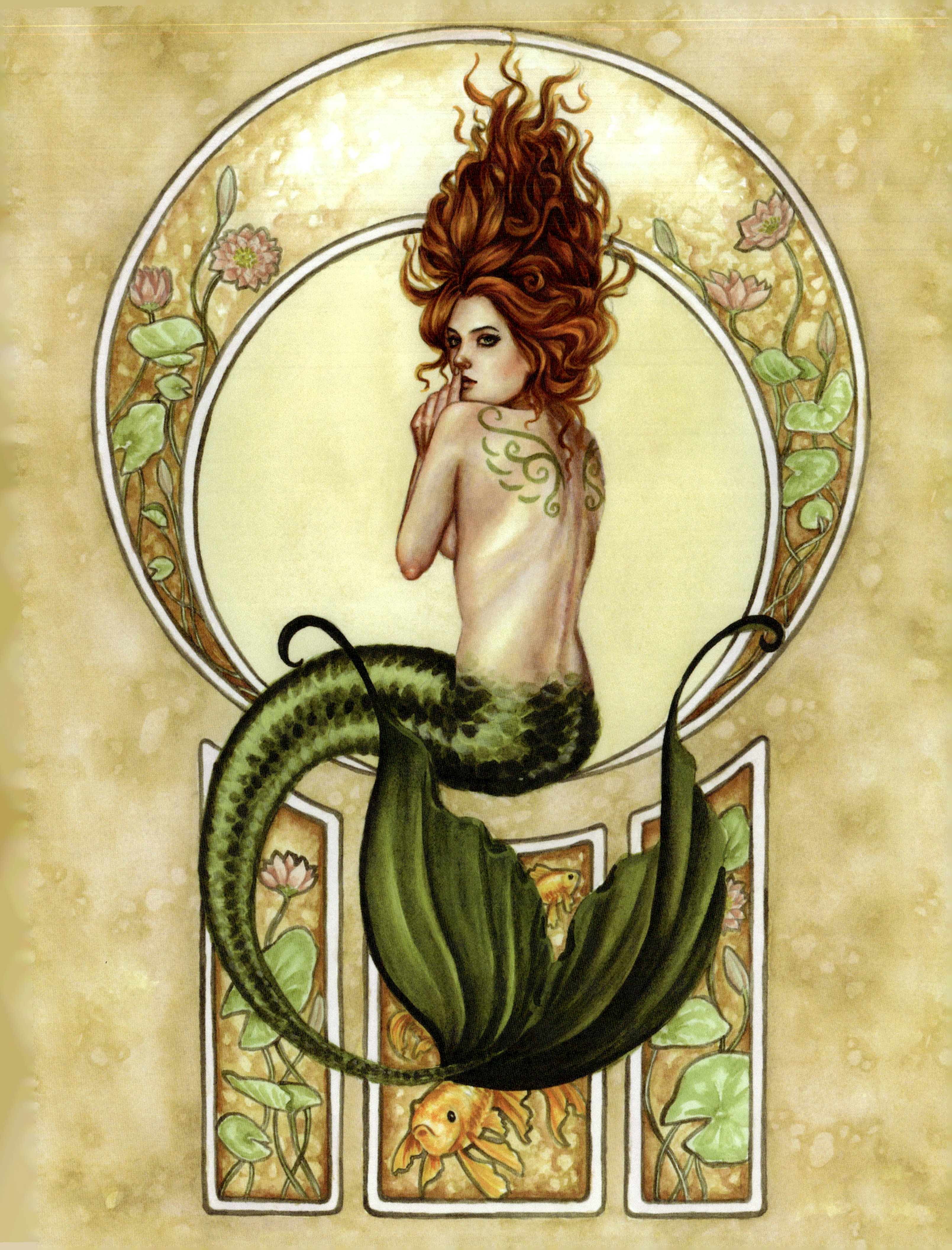

Moon Mermaid

Watercolour on watercolour paper, 2006

The moon and its effect on the ocean, creating tides, is a magical and powerful thing. It only makes sense that mermaids would worship the moon.

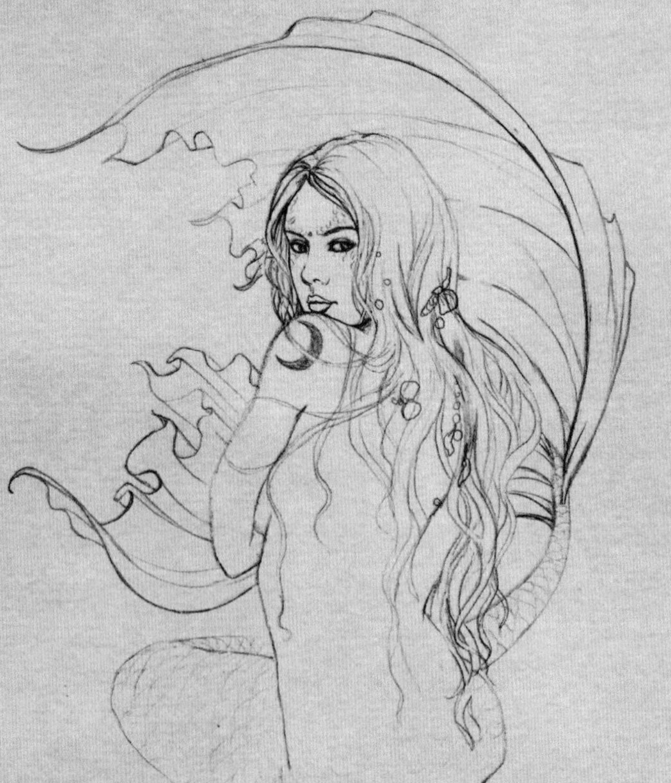

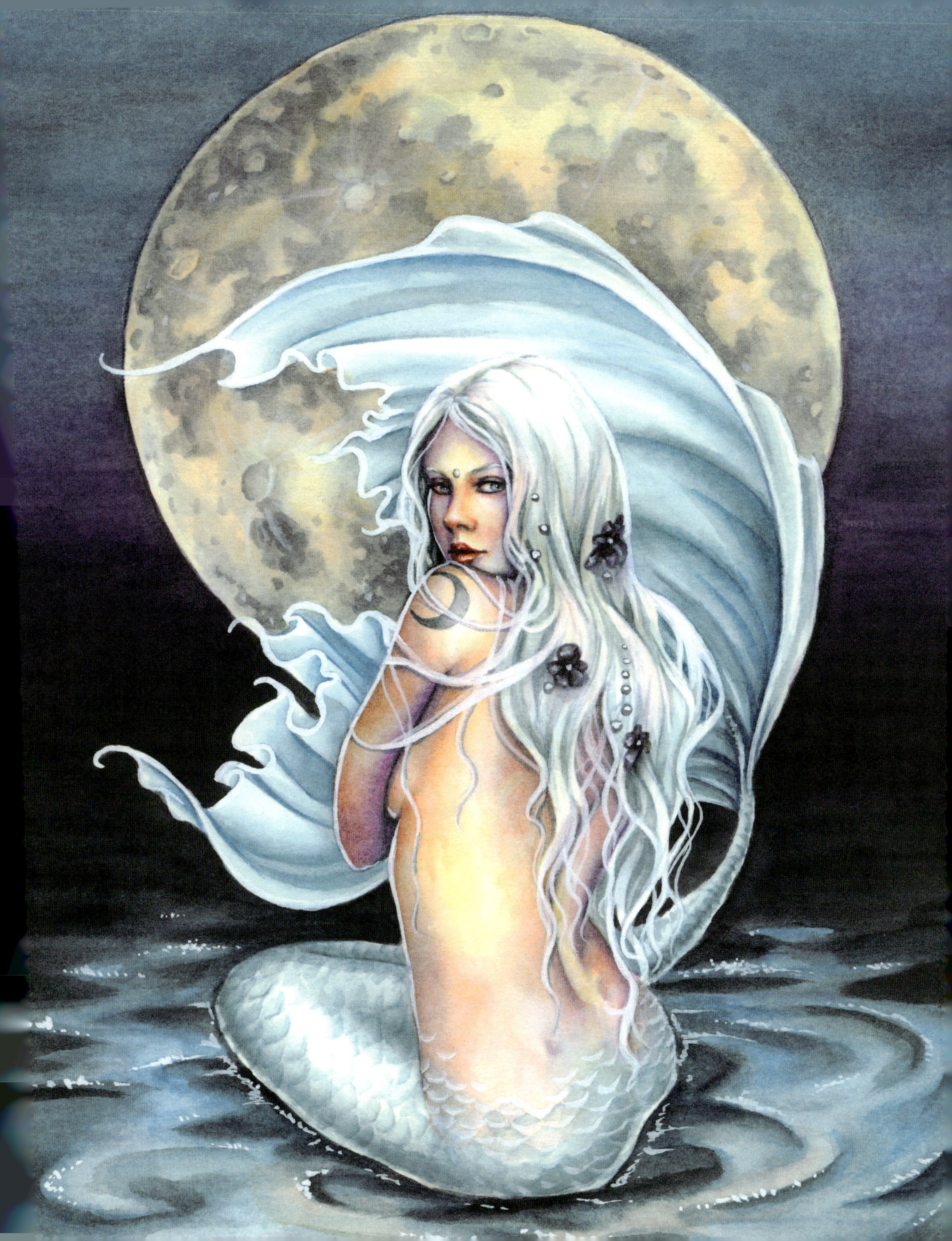

Treasures

Watercolour on watercolour paper, 2008

Mermaids are collectors, hoarders, of anything pretty or precious. This mermaid has gathered quite a collection of treasures.

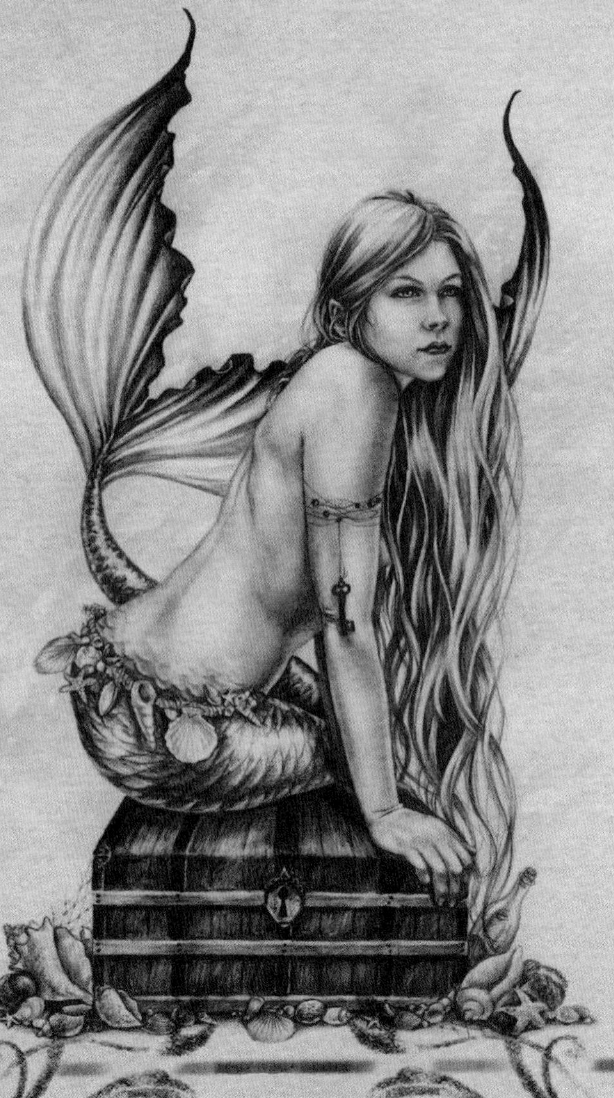

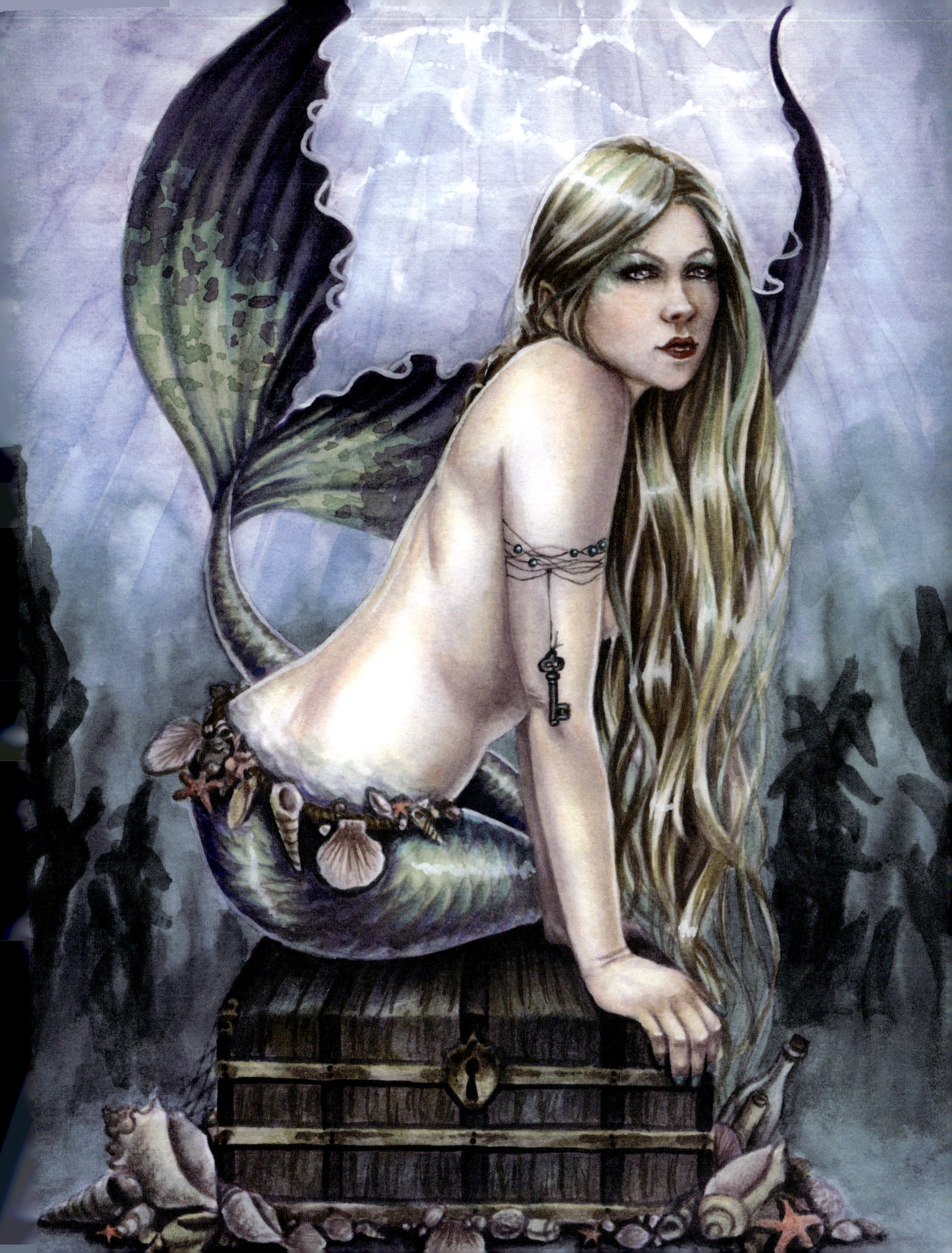

Motherhood

Digital (Photoshop and Wacom tablet), 2009

Possibly Selina's most famous and beloved artwork, Motherhood originated as a black and white pencil artwork (below), and only many years later after many requests did she create the coloured version to the right. Selina painted the original artwork in 2003 when she was 22 years old and single. In 2012, married with a new baby girl, everyone who sees the artwork for the first time comments that it looks just like Selina and her daughter.

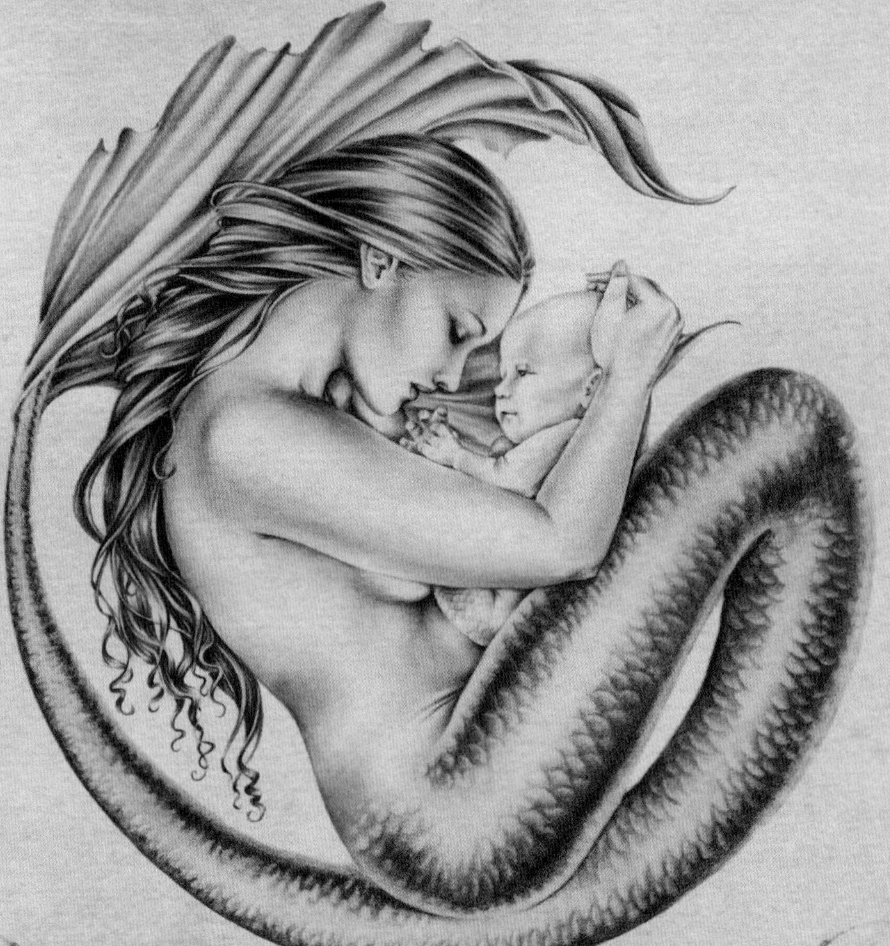

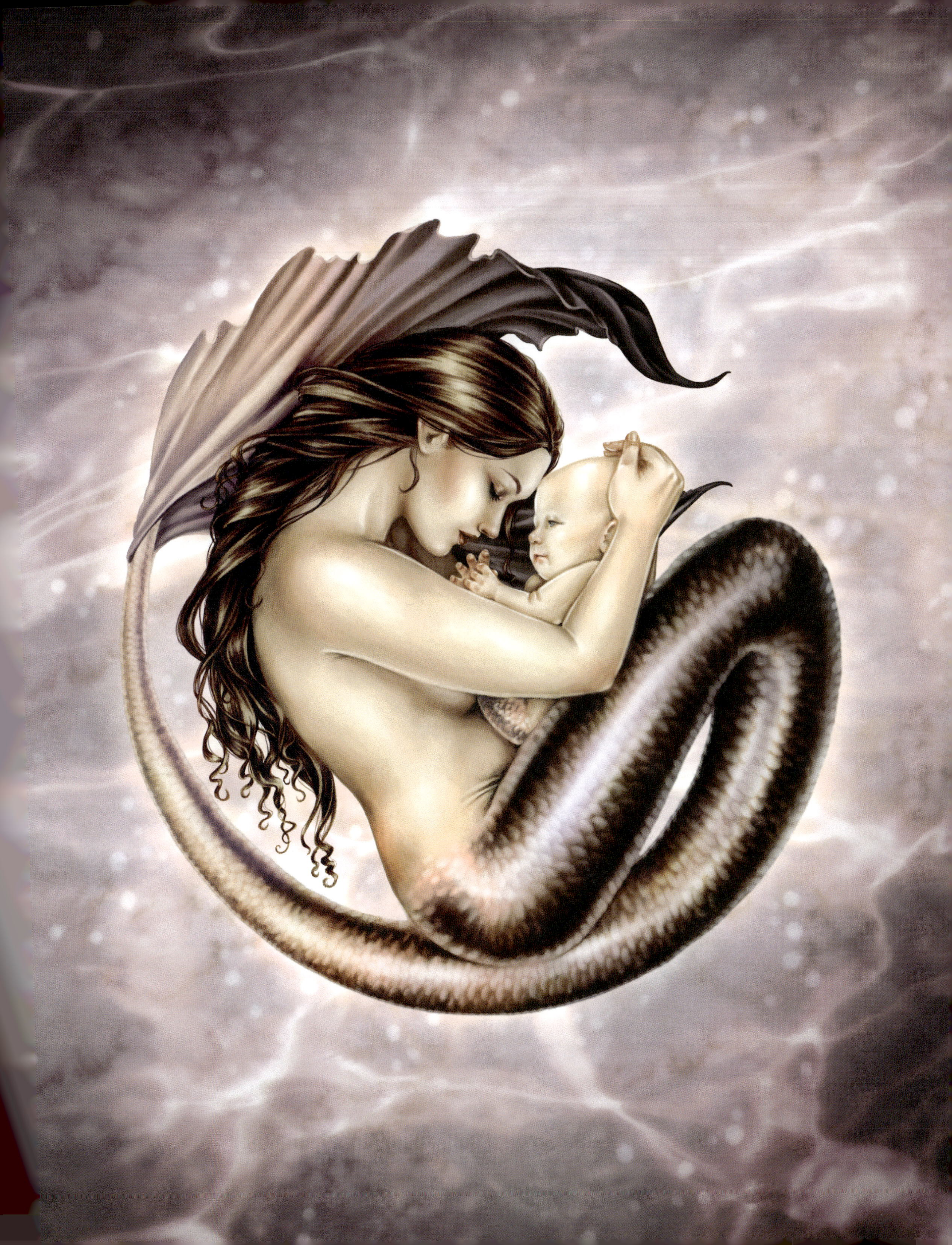

Sisters of the Sea

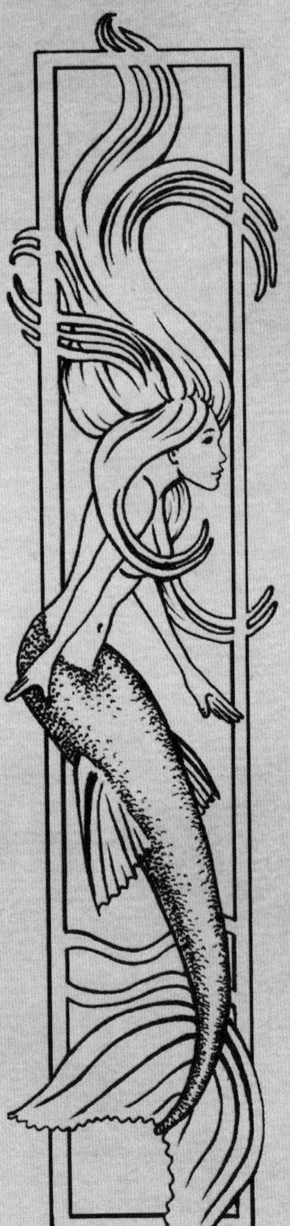

Mixed traditional mediums on paper, 2010

There is something very feminine about the concept of mermaids. While Selina does have a couple of mermen in her collection, mermaids are classically, and predominantly female.
These three mermaids may not be birth sisters, but they are sisters of the sea.

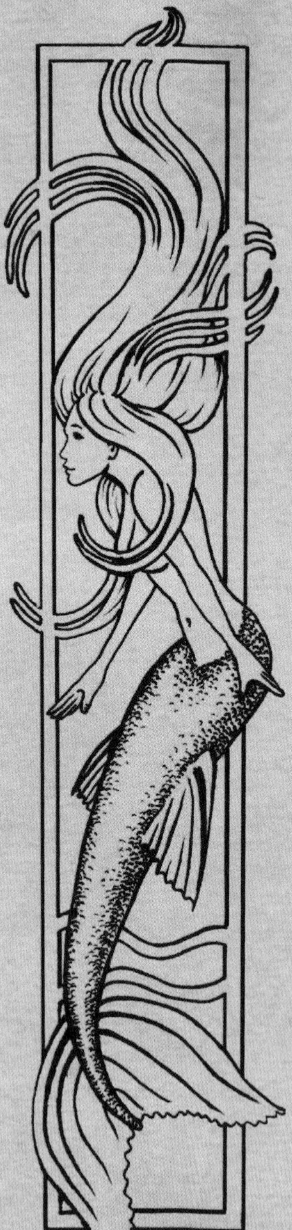

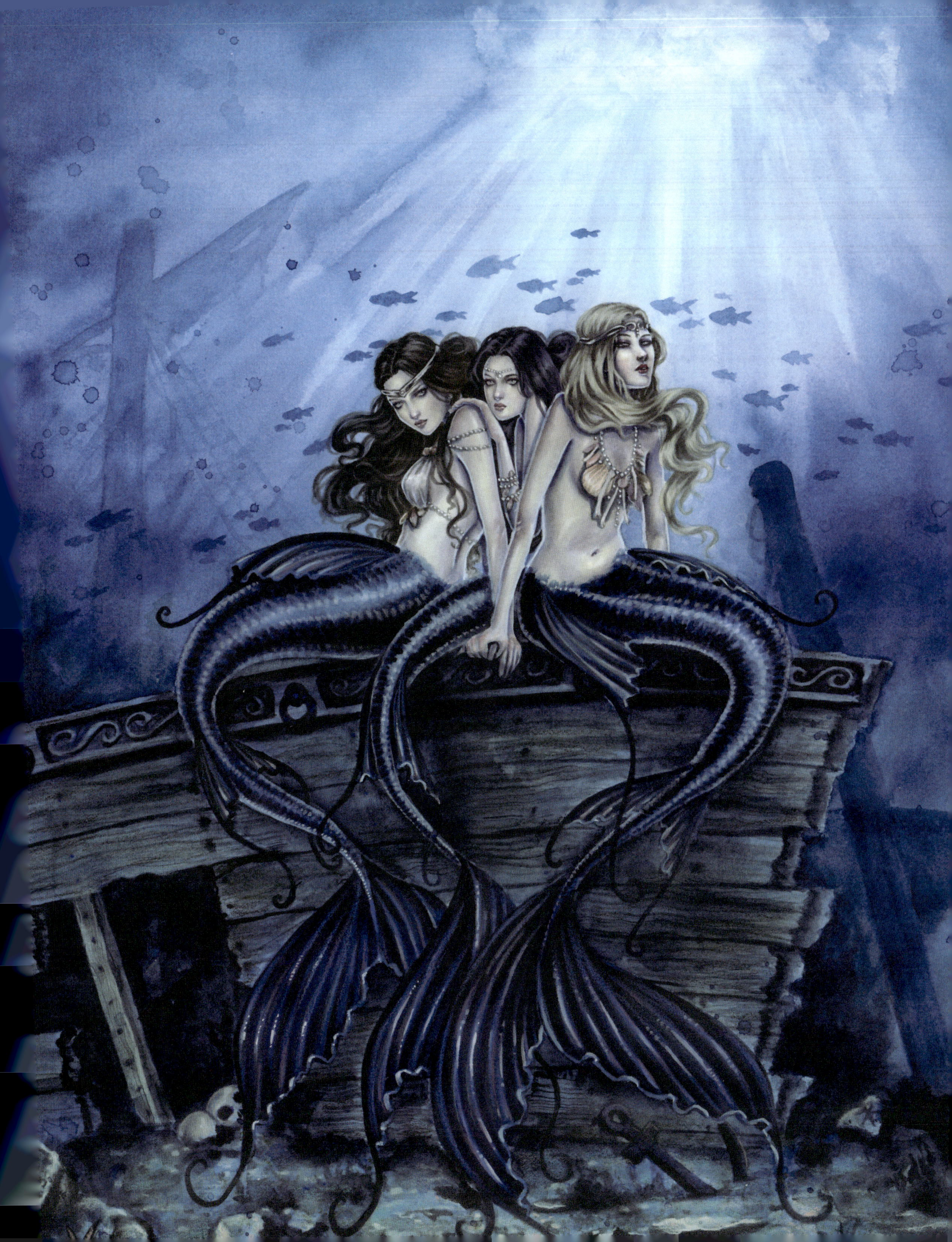

Washed Ashore

Mixed traditional mediums on illustration board, 2010

Selina began this artwork years before it was completed. She began painting it in watercolour on illustration board, but found the board did not hold the paint well in the methods she was used to. She returned to the half finished work later when she had developed new painting skills and methods, and completed it in acrylics and pencil.

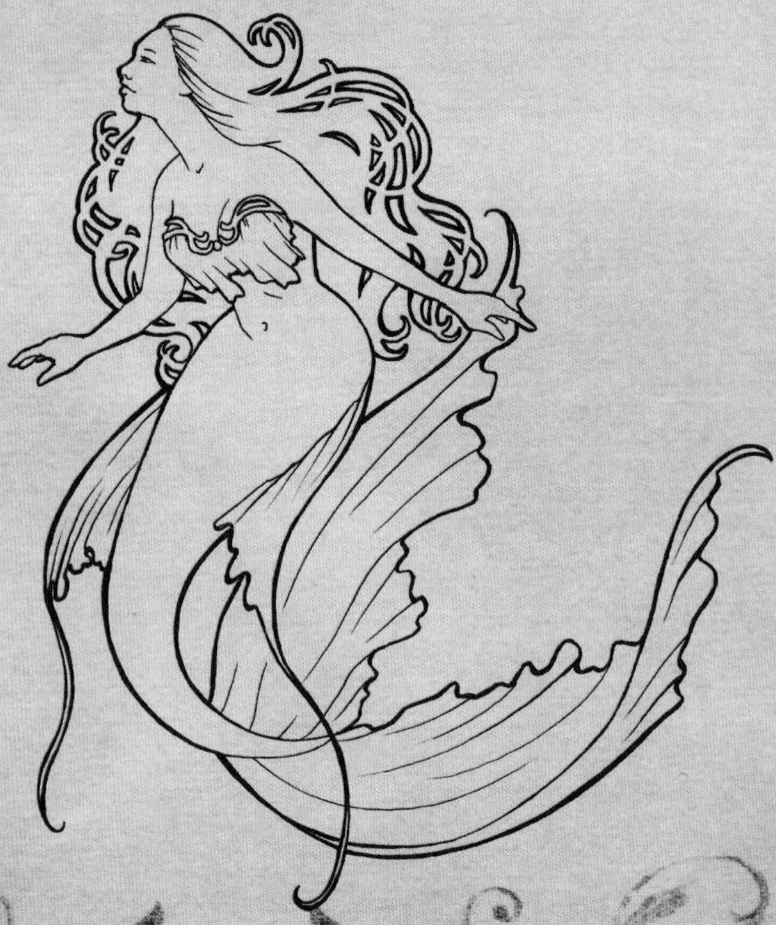

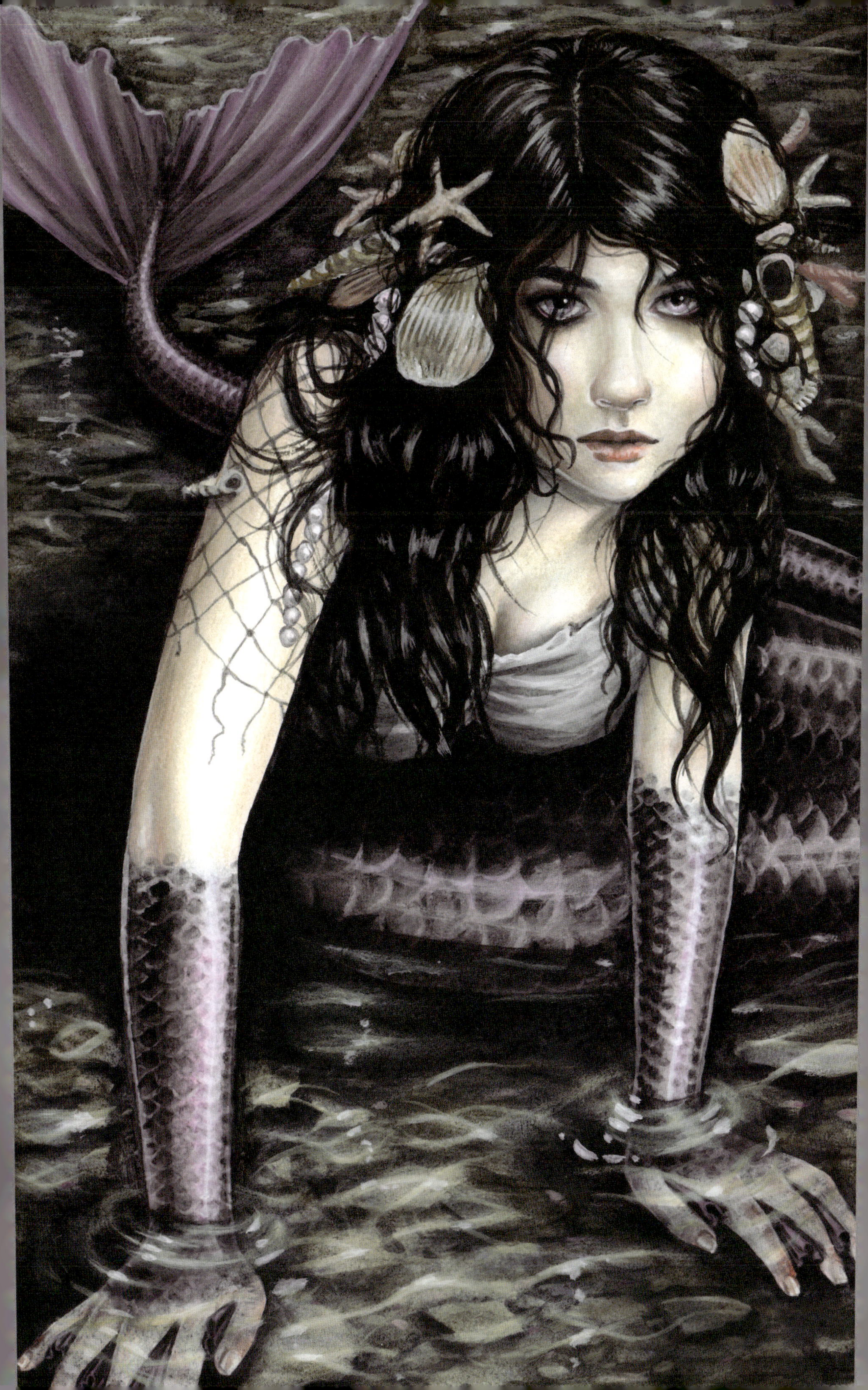

Sunlit Seas

Digital (Photoshop and Wacom tablet), 2012

This viking longboat must have gone far to have reached these tropical waters. In this digital artwork, Selina experimented with more painterly techniques and textures to create this seascape.

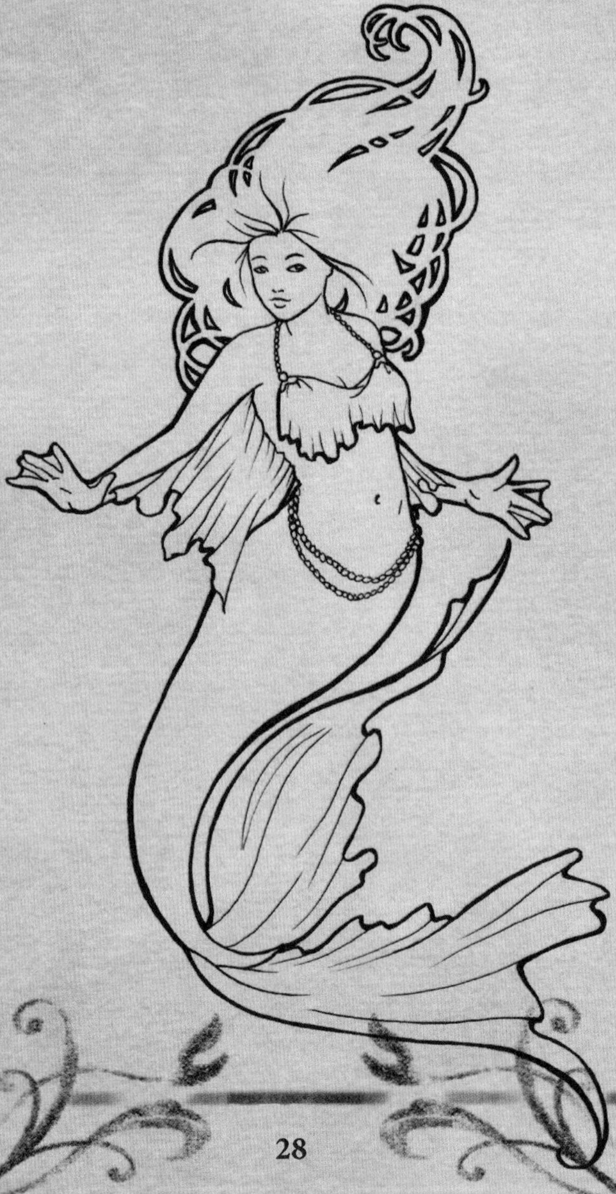

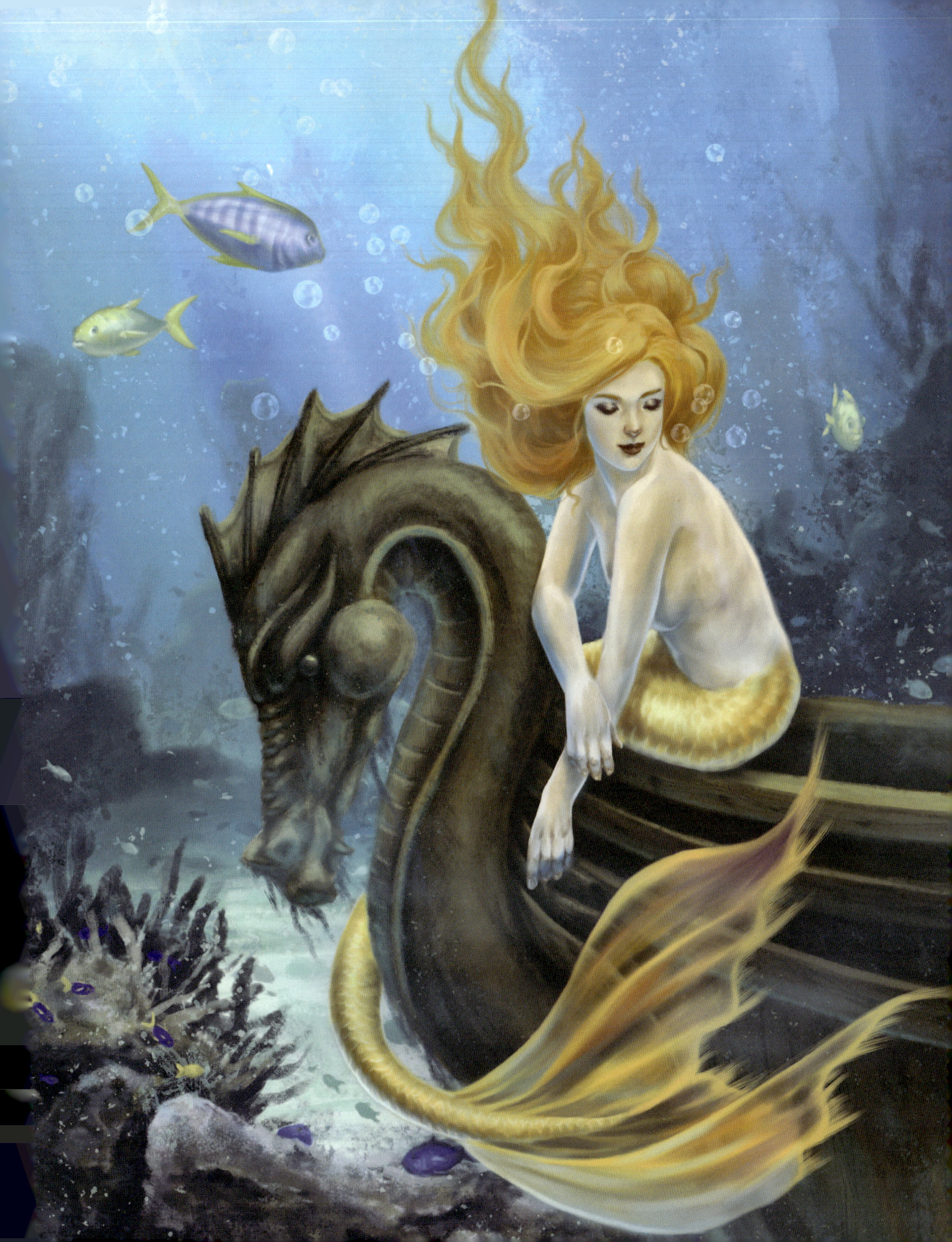

From Darkness

Digital (Photoshop and Wacom tablet), 2012

That which is beautiful is not always good. Selina's mermaids often have a dark side, as this one does, lurking in her shadowy cave.

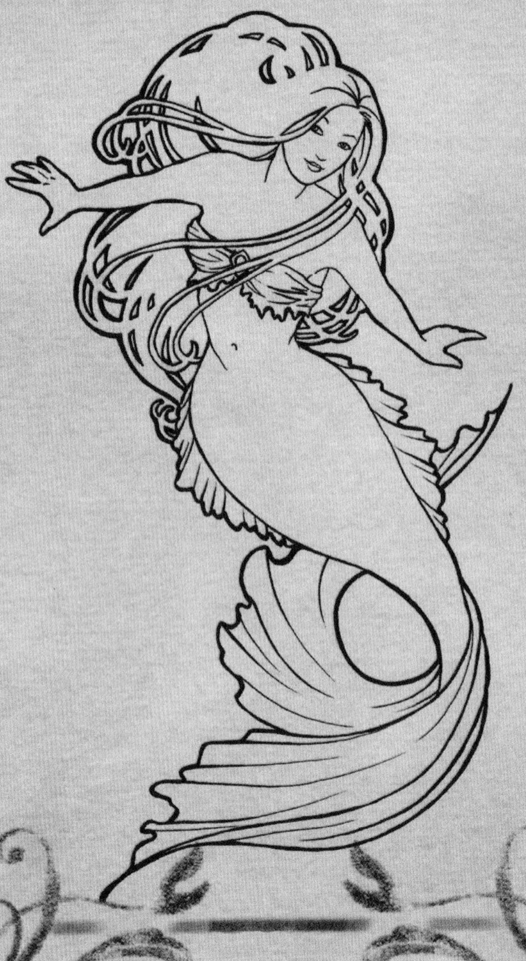

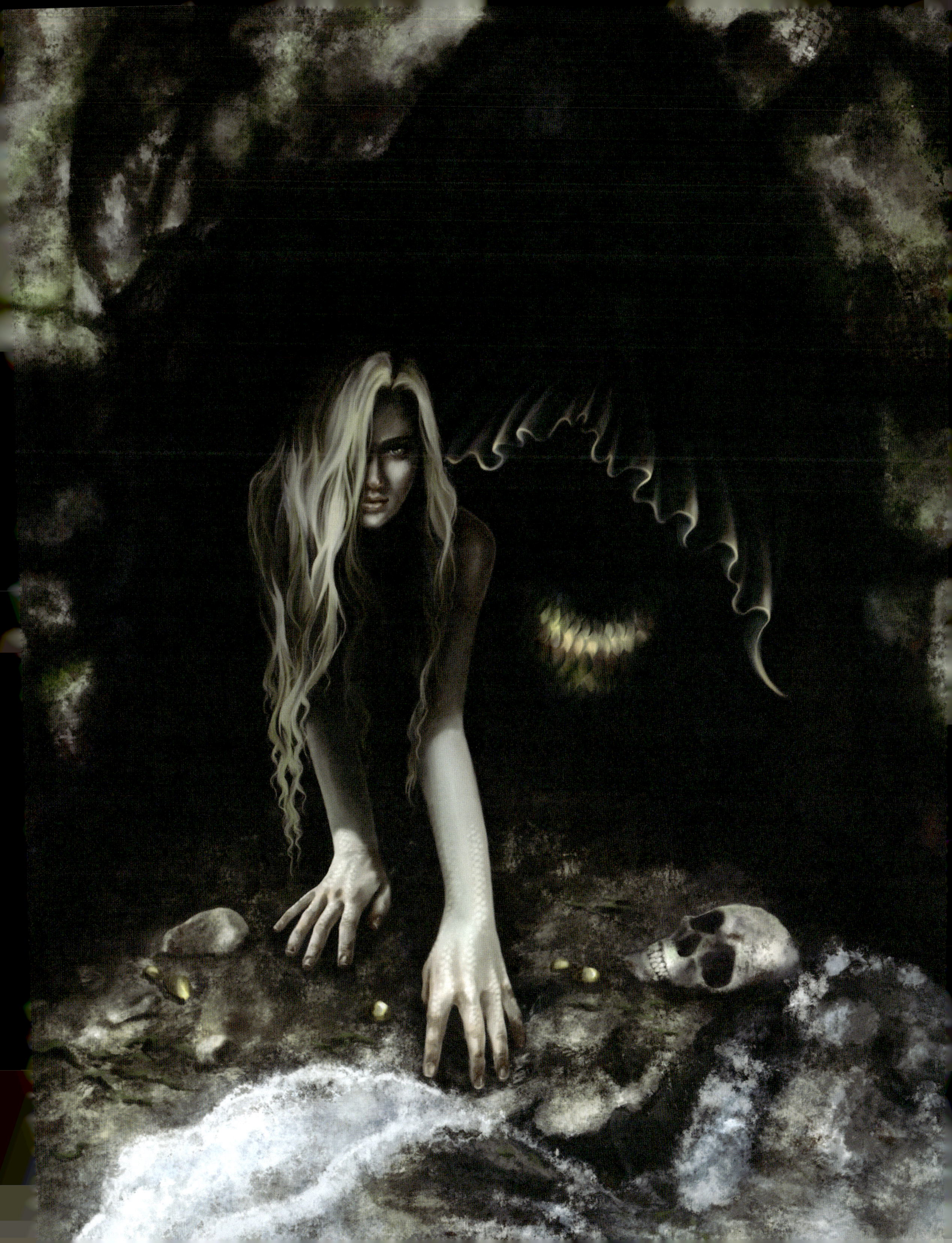

Special Delivery

Digital (Photoshop and Wacom tablet), 2012

Selina enjoys creating juxtaposition in her images, placing different, often opposing, elements against each other. In this artwork, it is the juxtaposition of the mermaid and the bird, and that the mermaid is also wearing clothing made of feathers. The fact the bird is carrying a small parcel for the mermaid adds further interest, a story waiting to be told.

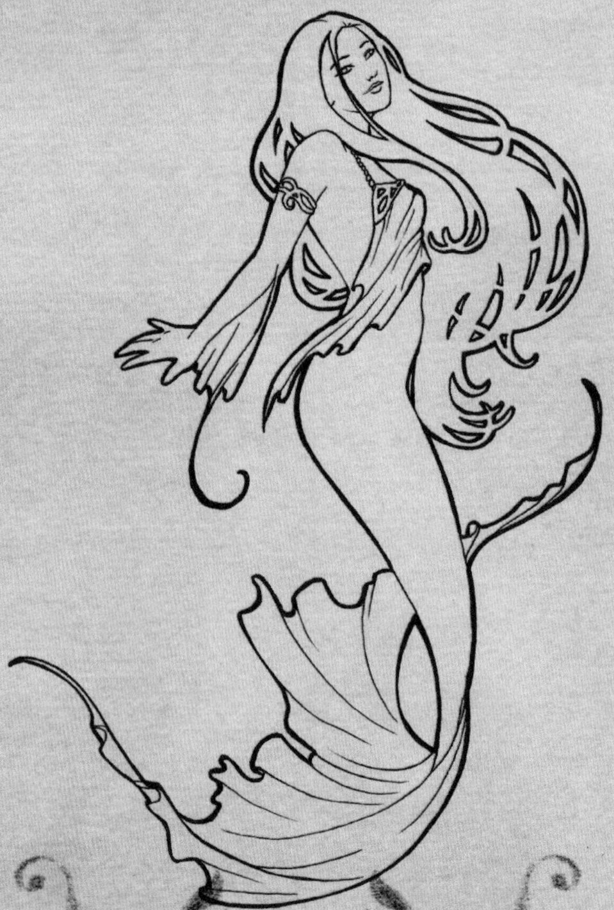

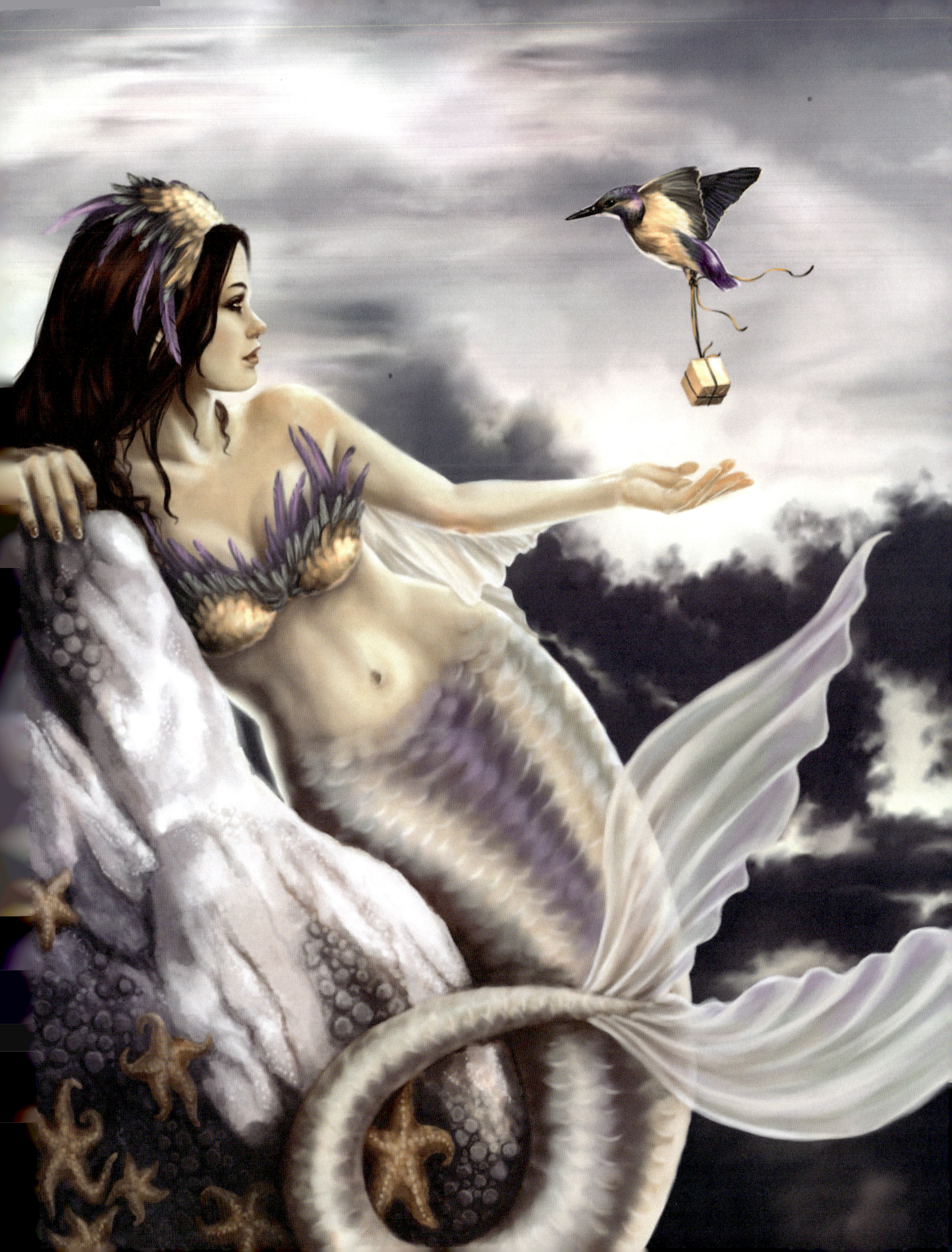

Impossible Love

Watercolours on watercolour paper, 2006

Selina created the first version of this image in 1998 when she was in high school (below). It became one of her most popular images, but she was never happy with the technical quality of it. Years later she painted a new version of the same concept which still remains one of her most favourite artworks.

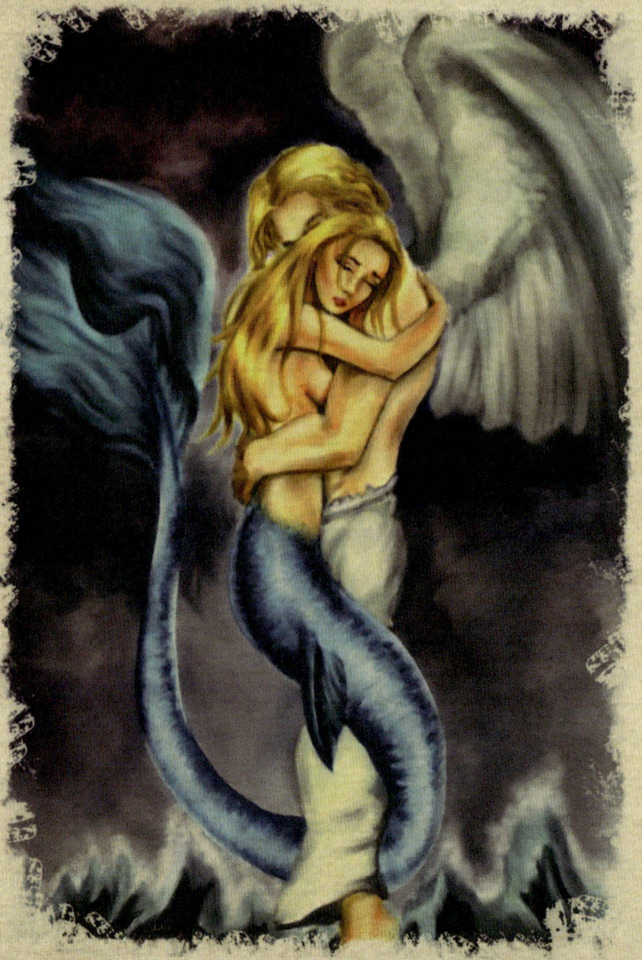

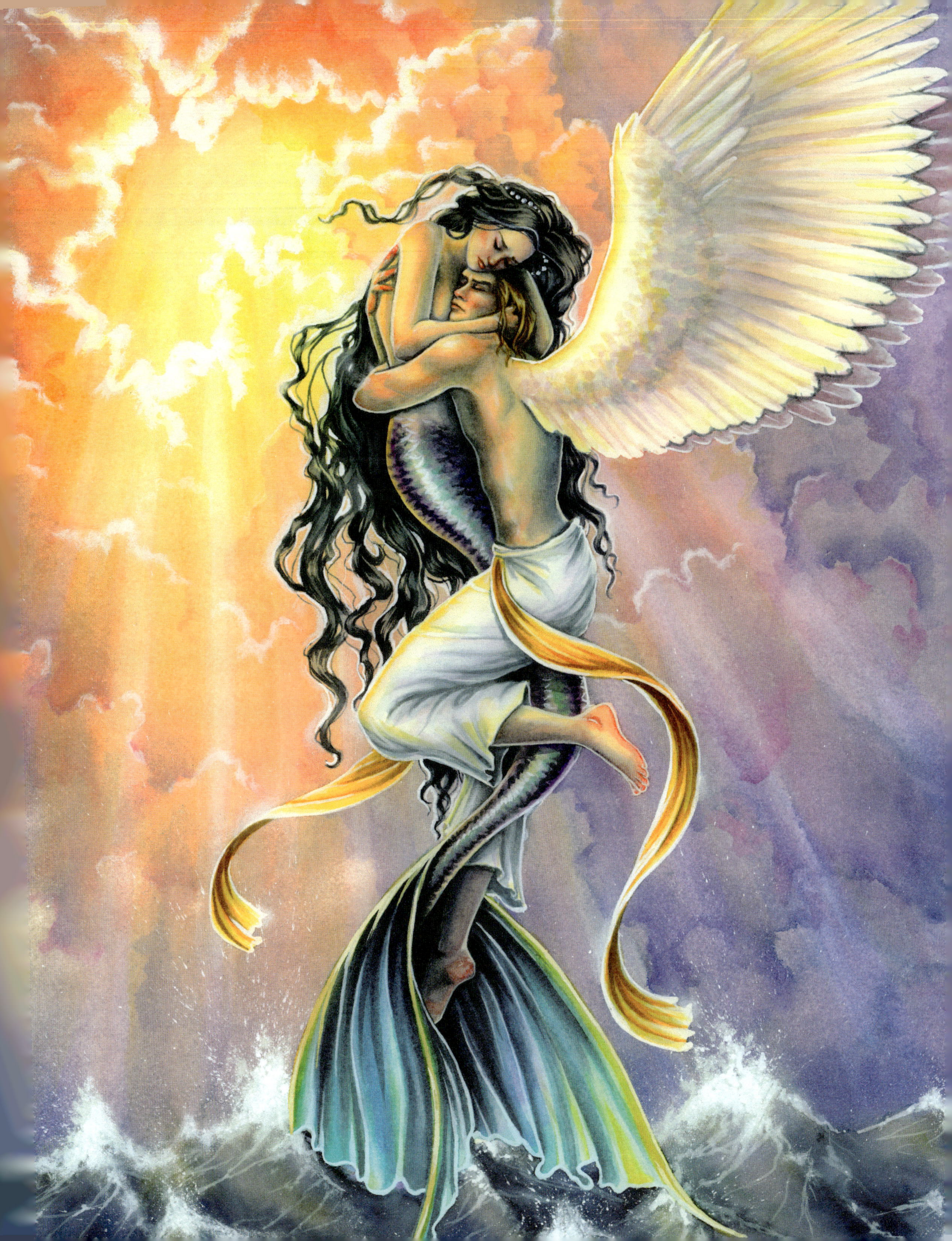

Dark Waters

Watercolour on watercolour paper, 2005

This artwork is the bottom section of a vertical triptych, a three part artwork with fairies in the sky at the top, waves in the centre, and mermaids below. At the time, it was the most detailed and complicated artwork Selina had painted and is still a close tie in that regard.

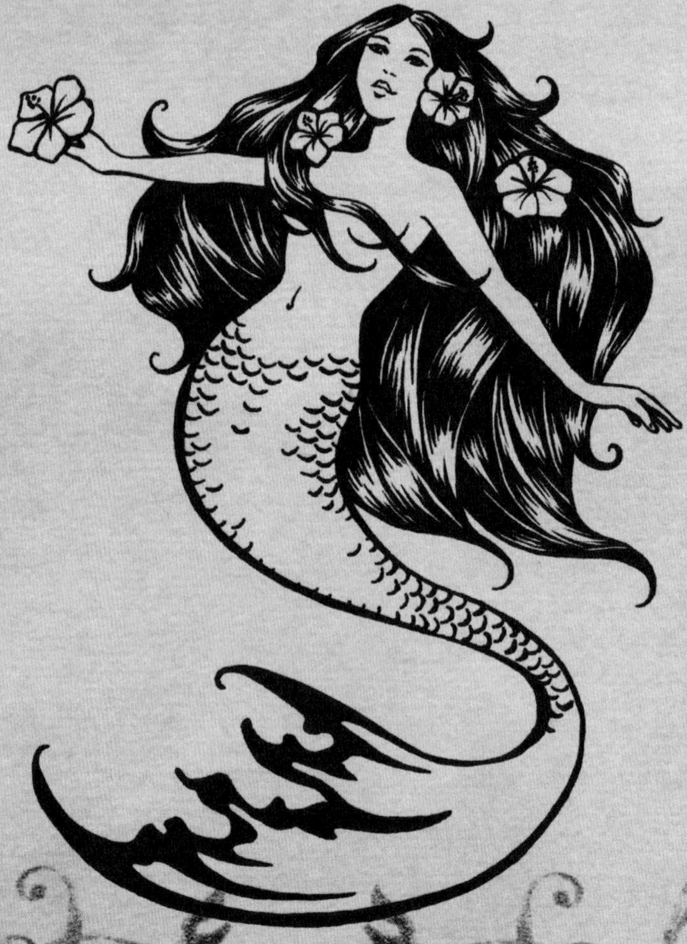

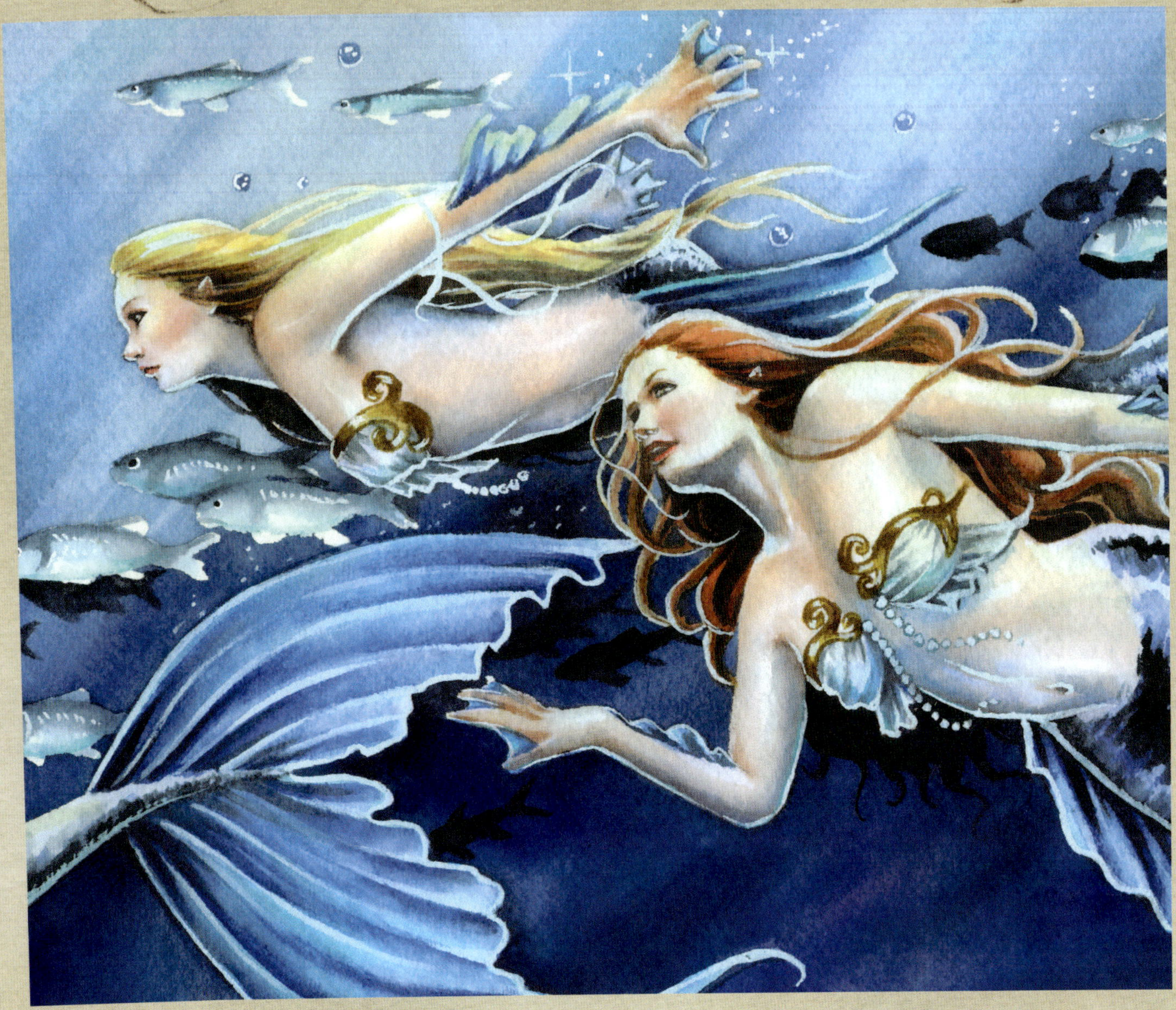

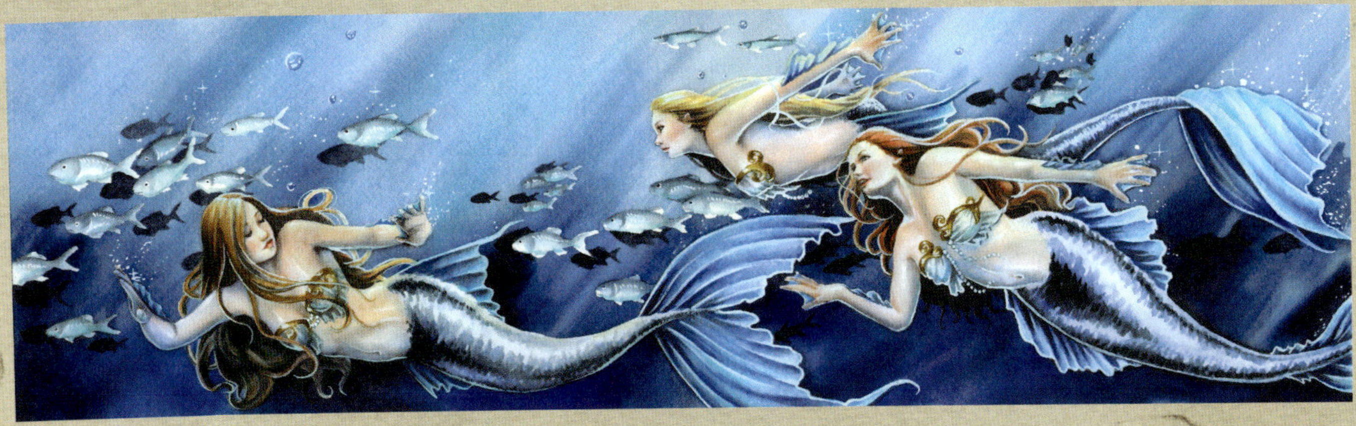

Mirror, Mirror

Digital (Photoshop and Wacom tablet), 2012

While the majority of Selina's mermaids, fairies and other characters are Caucasian, she does hope to include more fantasy beings of different ethnicities into her collection. This Asian mermaid gazes at her reflection in the water surface. To give the artwork a surreal effect, the water surface is vertical rather than horizontal, and lotus blossoms float underwater.

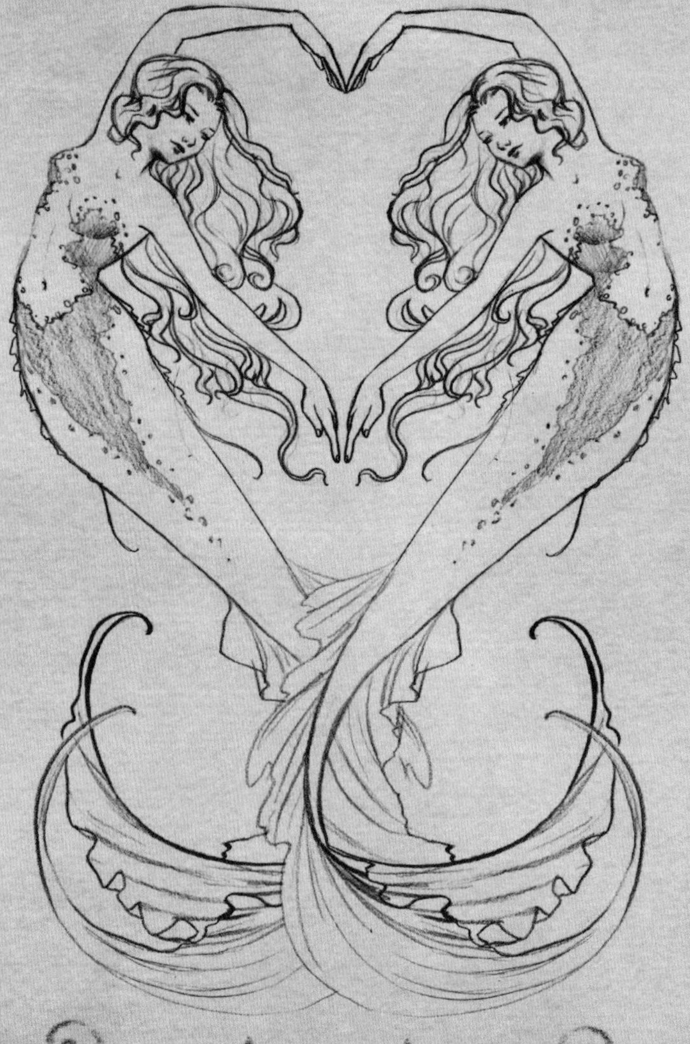

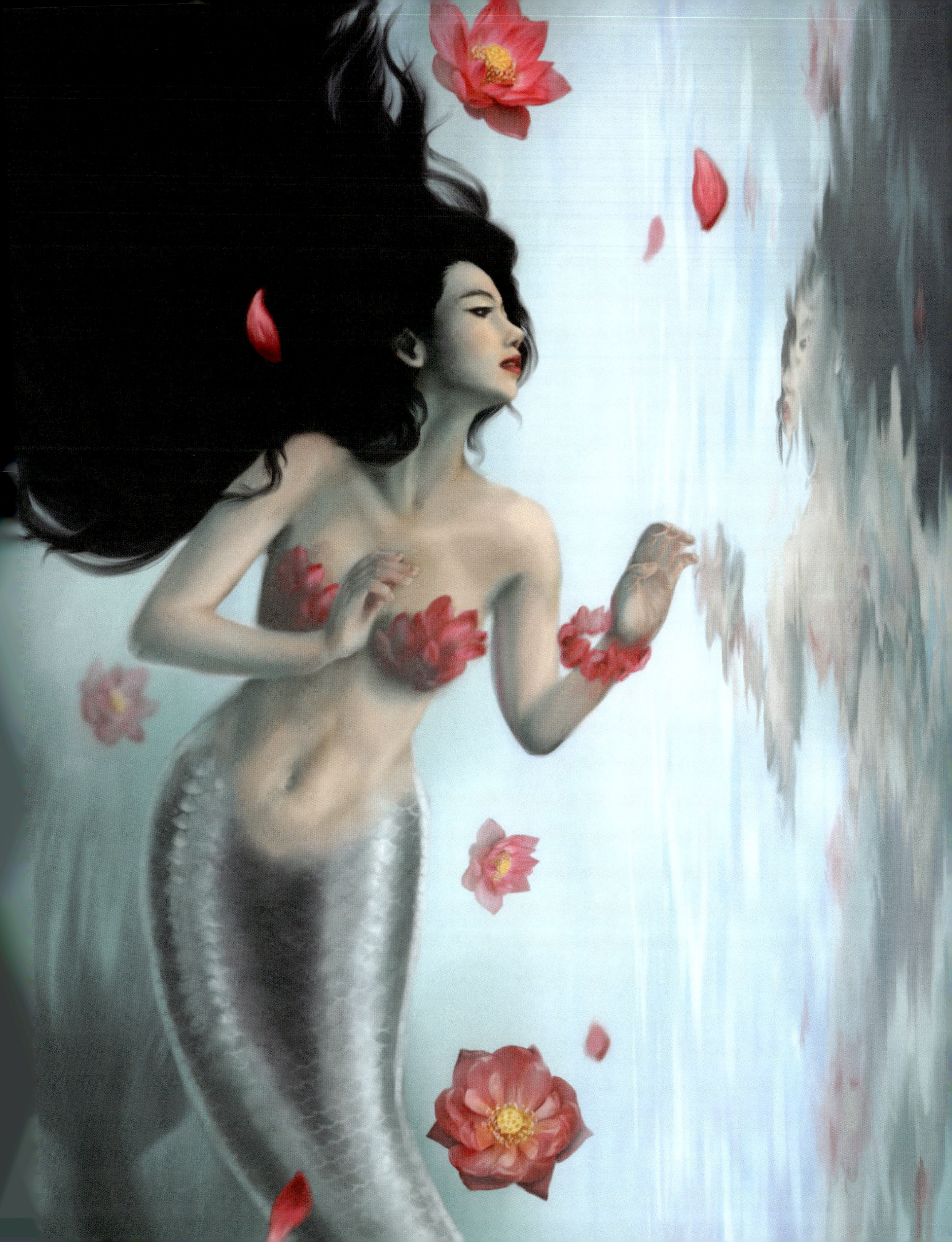

Air

Digital (Photoshop and Wacom tablet), 2012

One of Selina's favourite movies from her childhood was "Splash" with Tom Hanks and Darryl Hannah. It begins with Tom Hanks lost at sea and mermaids share breath with him to stop him from drowning. This is Selina's version of that concept, and to show that not all mermaids wish to drown men.

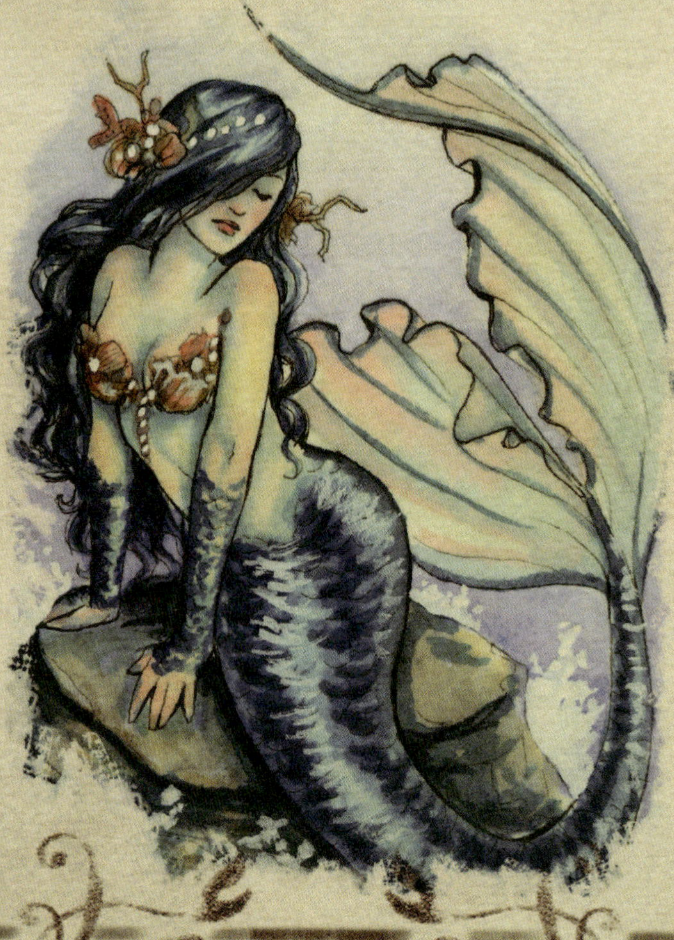

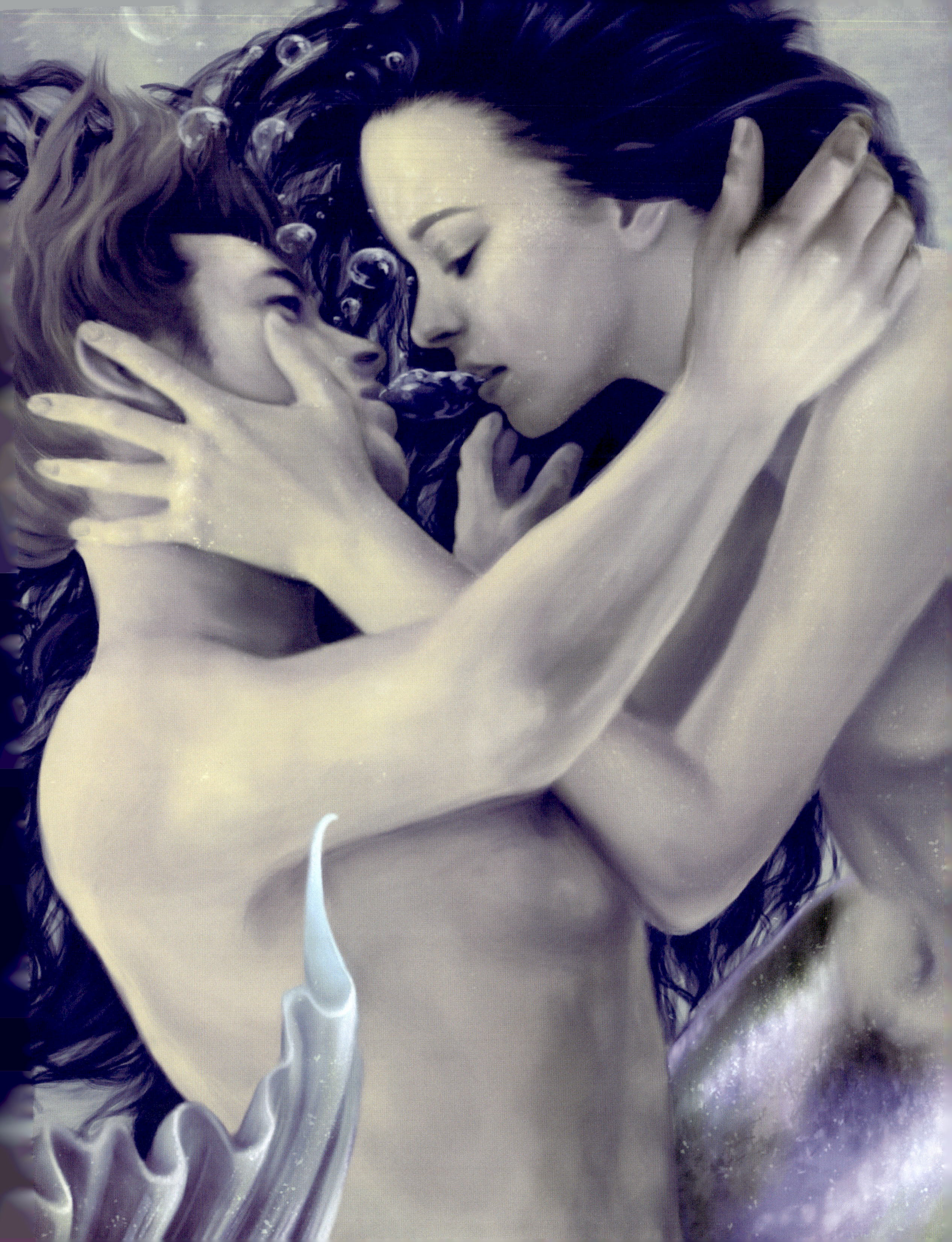

Sea of Roses

Digital (Photoshop and Wacom tablet), 2011

Mermaids are sensual creatures, and this one is no exception. She lies in a sea of roses instead of water. The whole image is about love and passion, and is a remake of an earlier version.

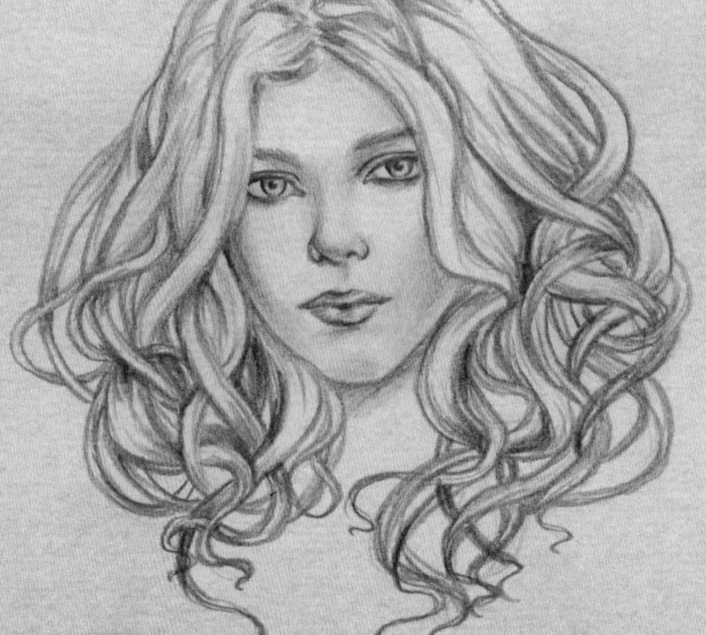

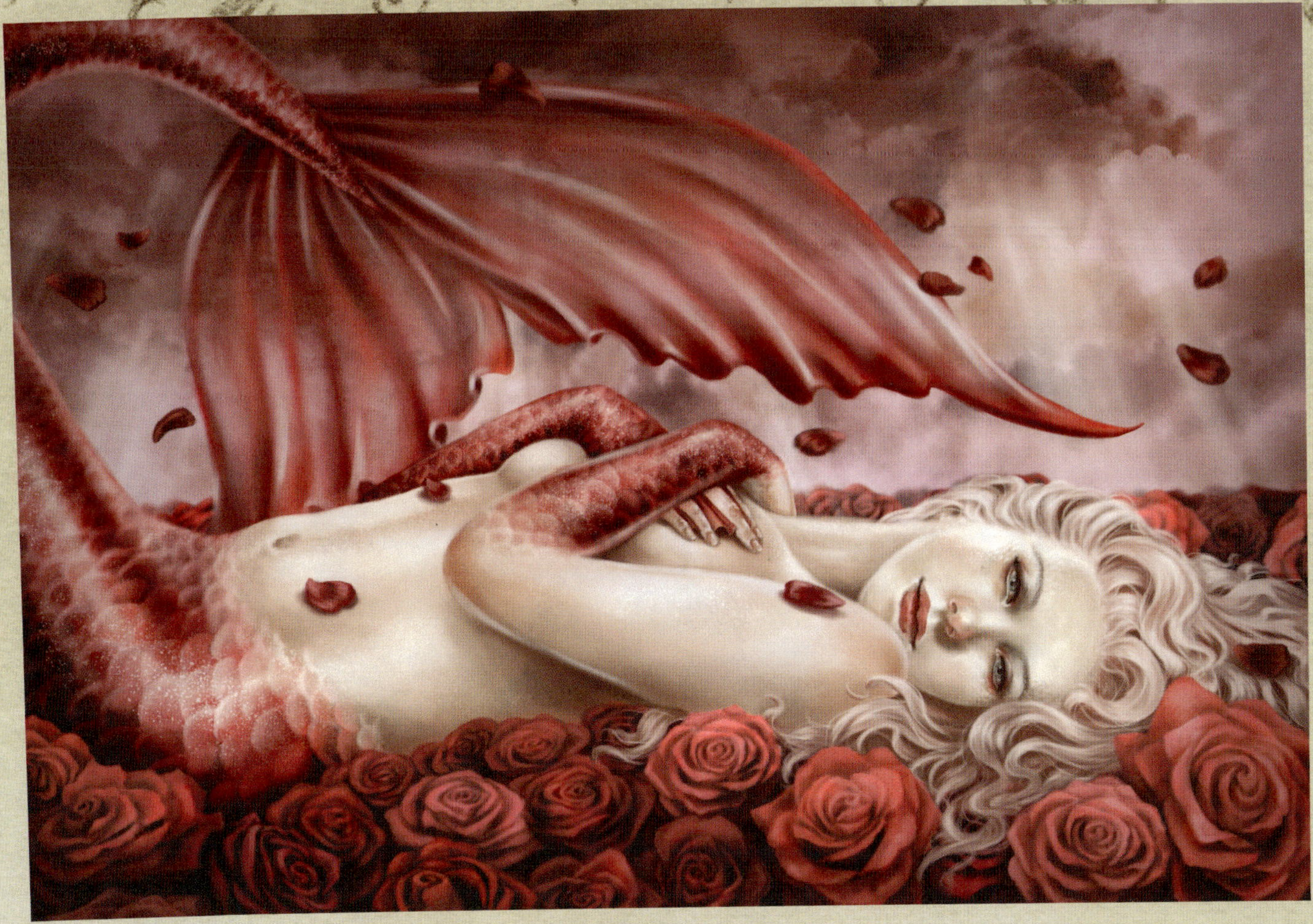

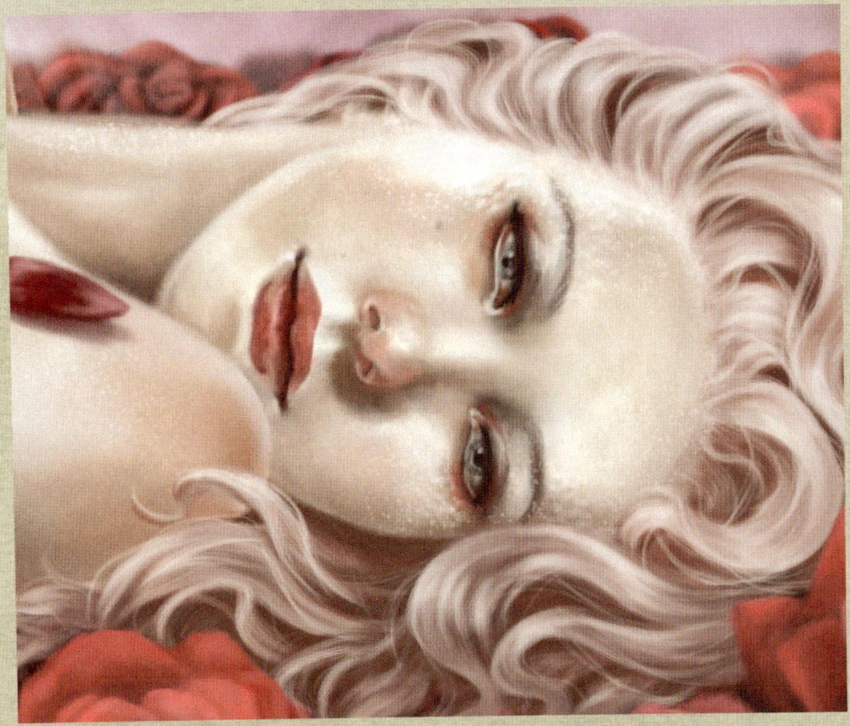

A Mermaid's Loss

Digital (Photoshop and Wacom tablet), 2012

Selina's version of the classic scene from the little mermaid, where the mermaid saves a drowning man from a shipwreck. Whether the man survives or not, the mermaid knows she will lose him either way and cannot be with him.

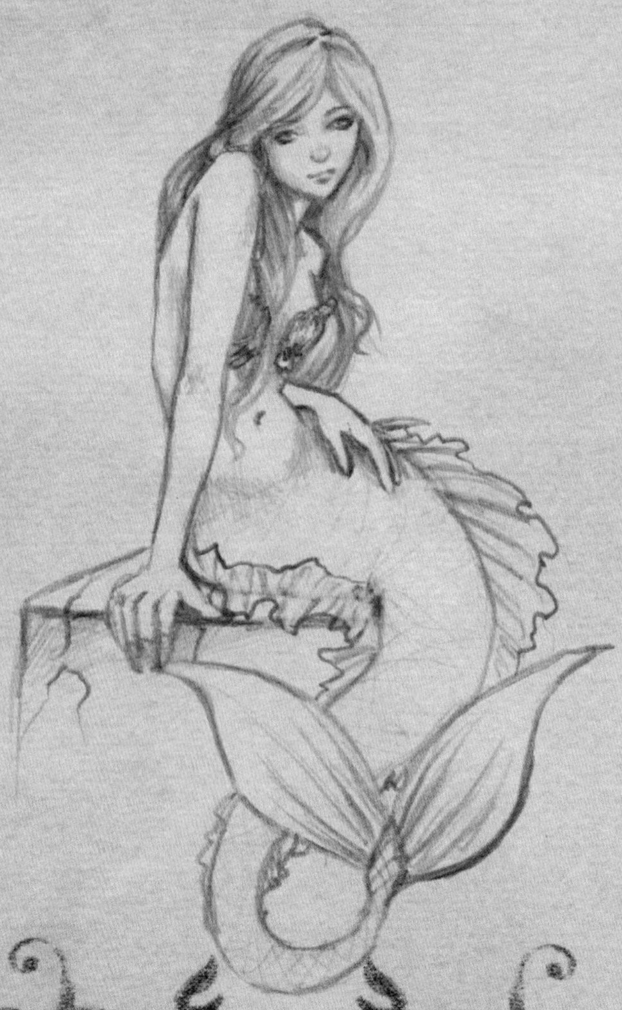

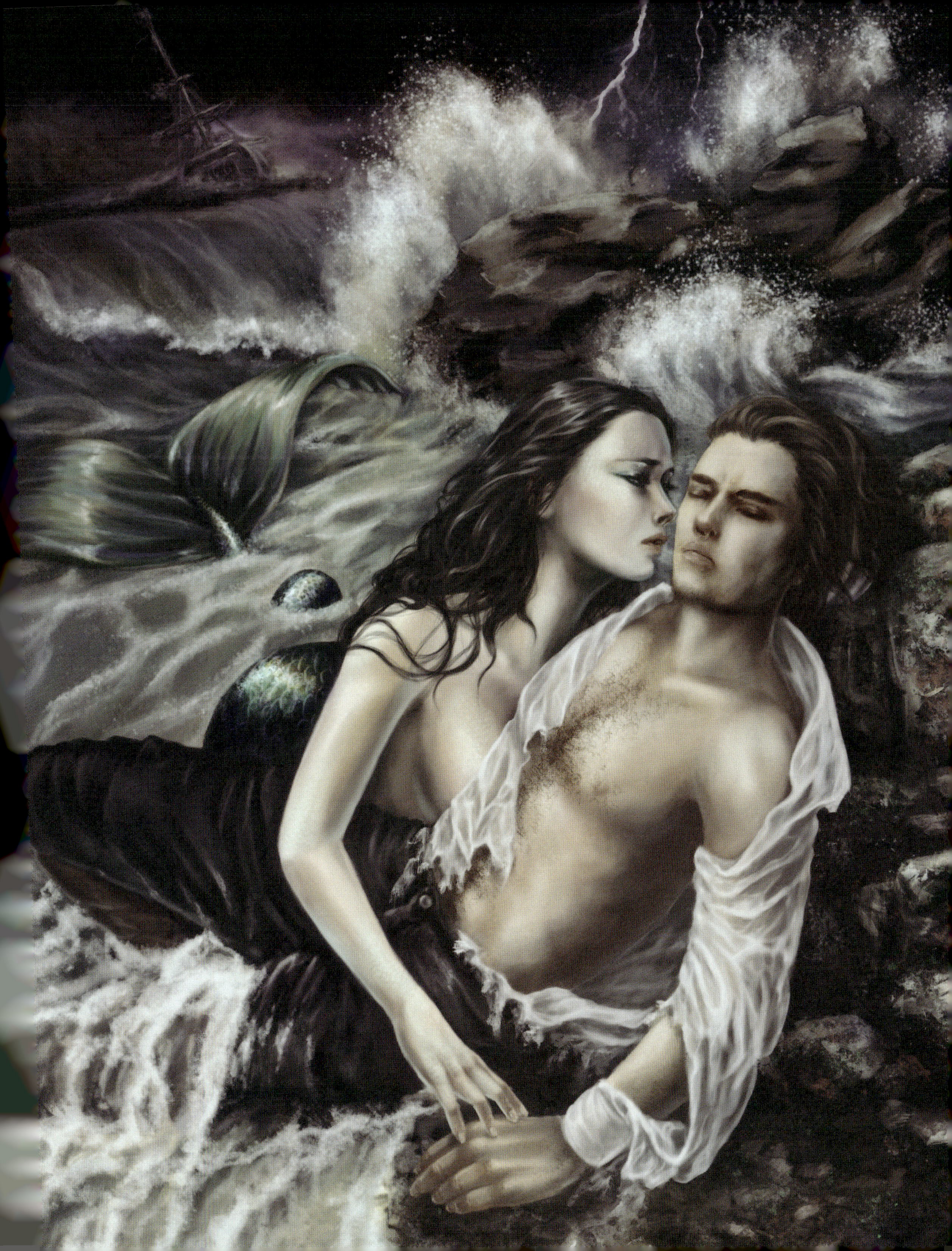

Lily

Digital (Photoshop and Wacom tablet), 2012

One of Selina's favourite artworks from her collection, the style and colour palette are reminiscent of her favourite era of art- the Pre-Raphaelites. The mermaid herself is intended to be of mixed Asian appearance.

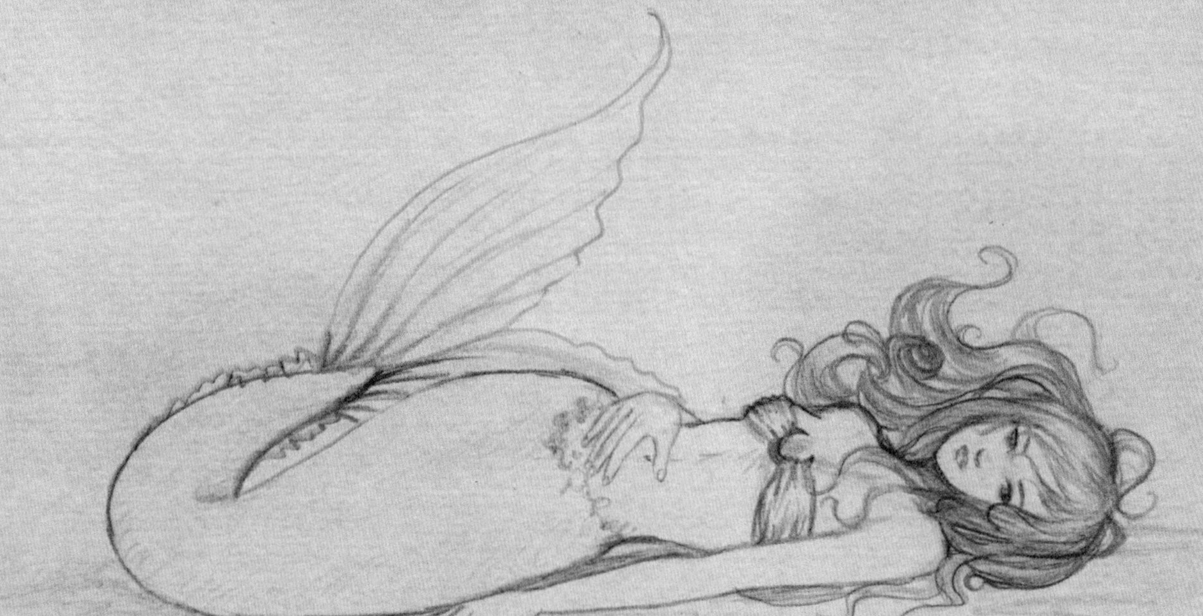

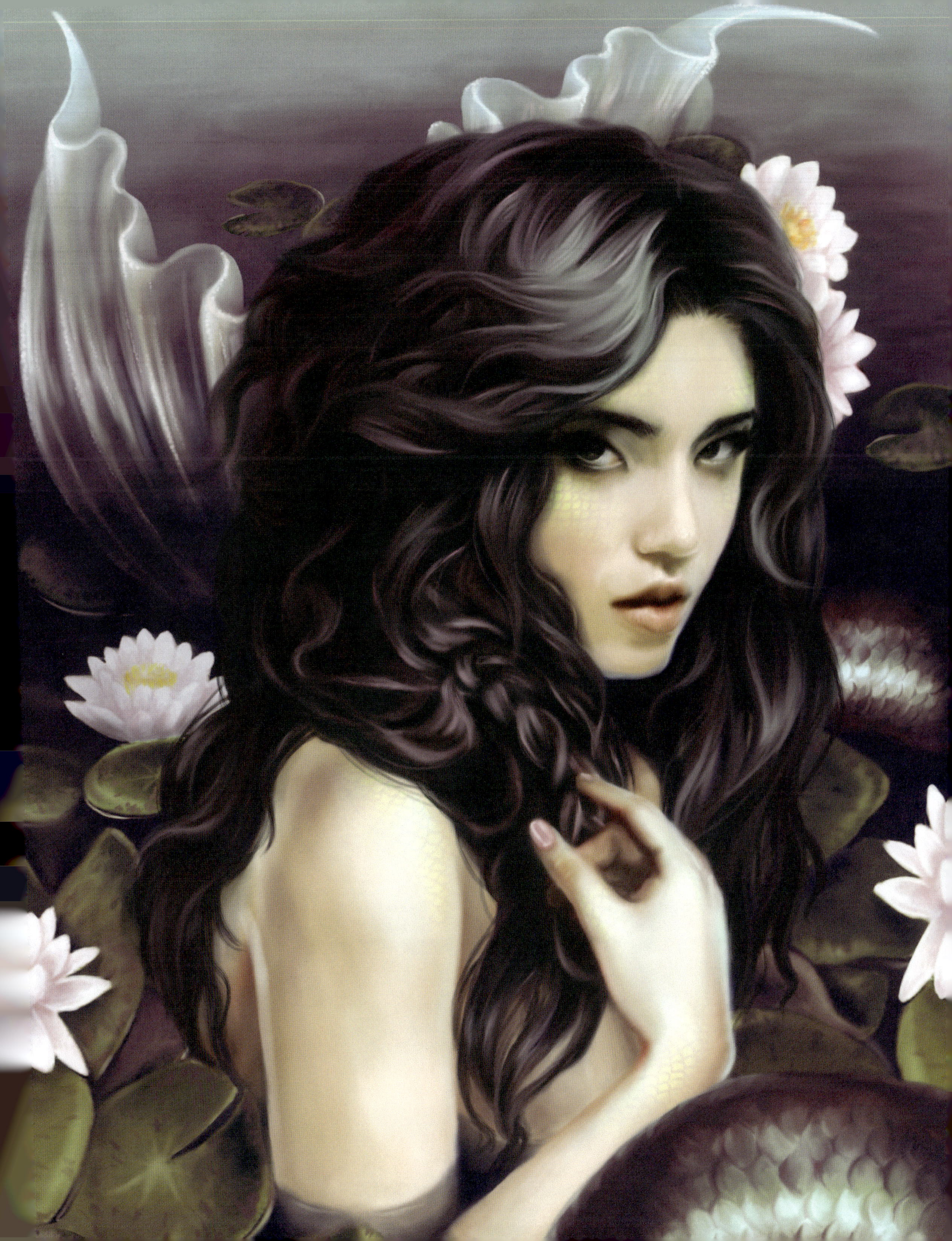

Selkie

Digital (Photoshop and Wacom tablet), 2012

Selkies are slightly different to classic mermaids. From Irish mythology, they are creatures who look like seals, but can take off their seal skin and become beautiful women. In this artwork Selina shows a Selkie removing her skin, in the process of becoming human but still with the seal tail. The woman keeps some of the seal's spots on her skin.

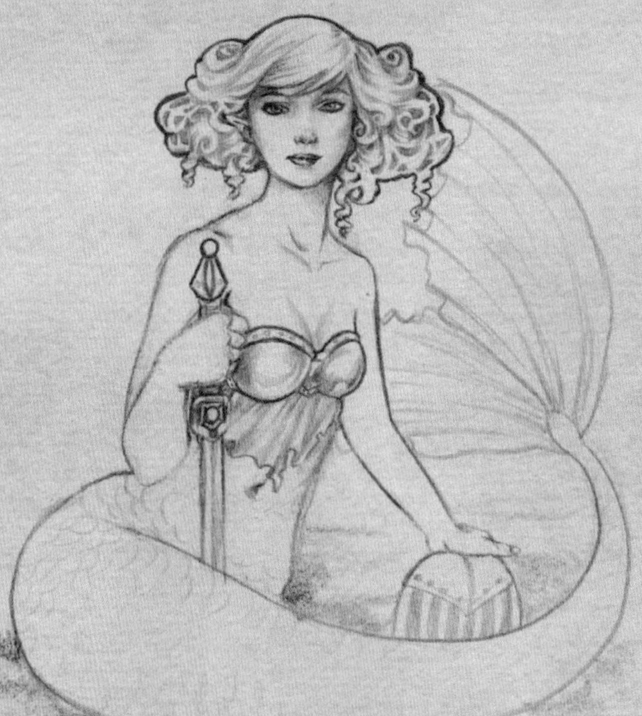

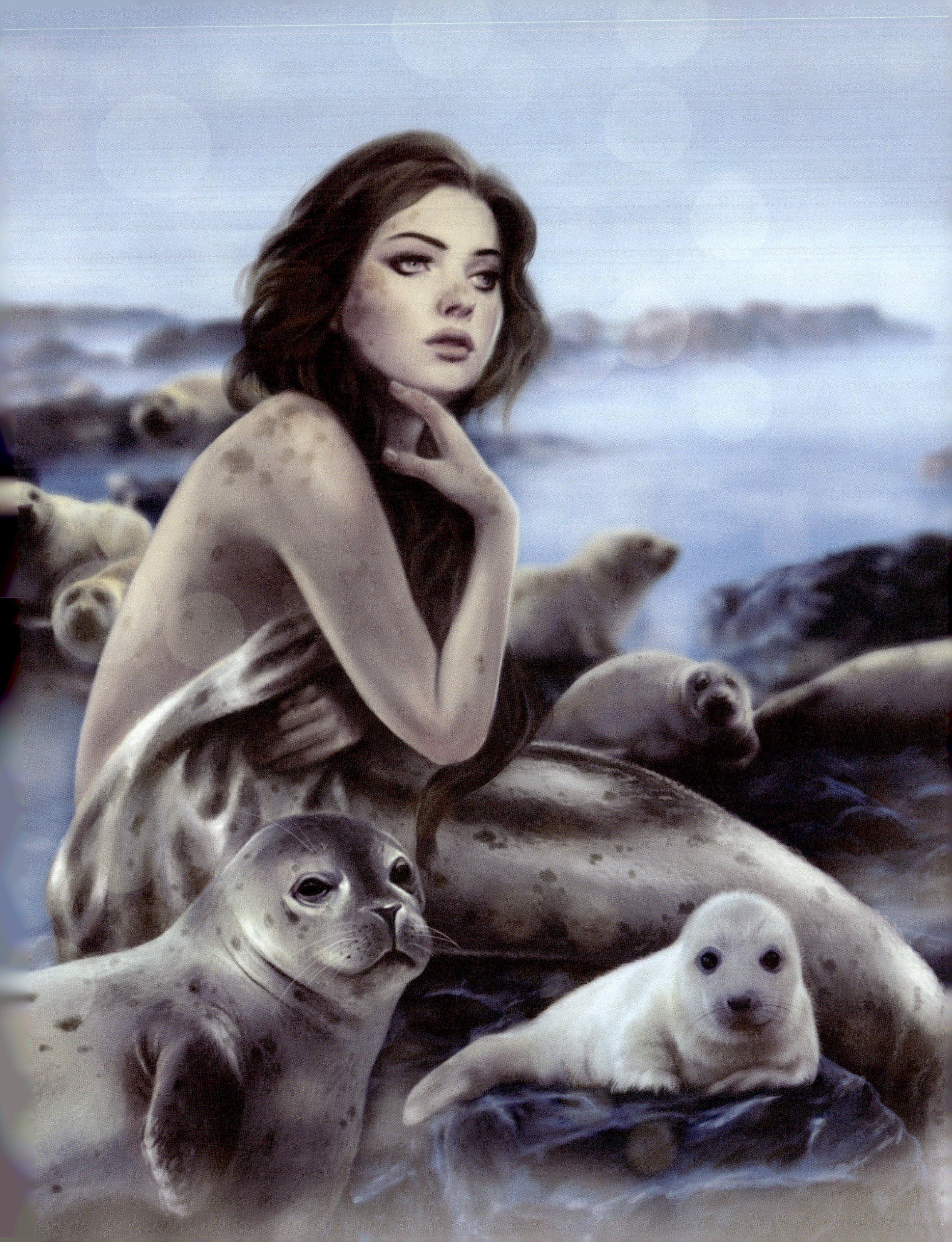

Source of Power

Digital (Photoshop and Wacom tablet), 2012

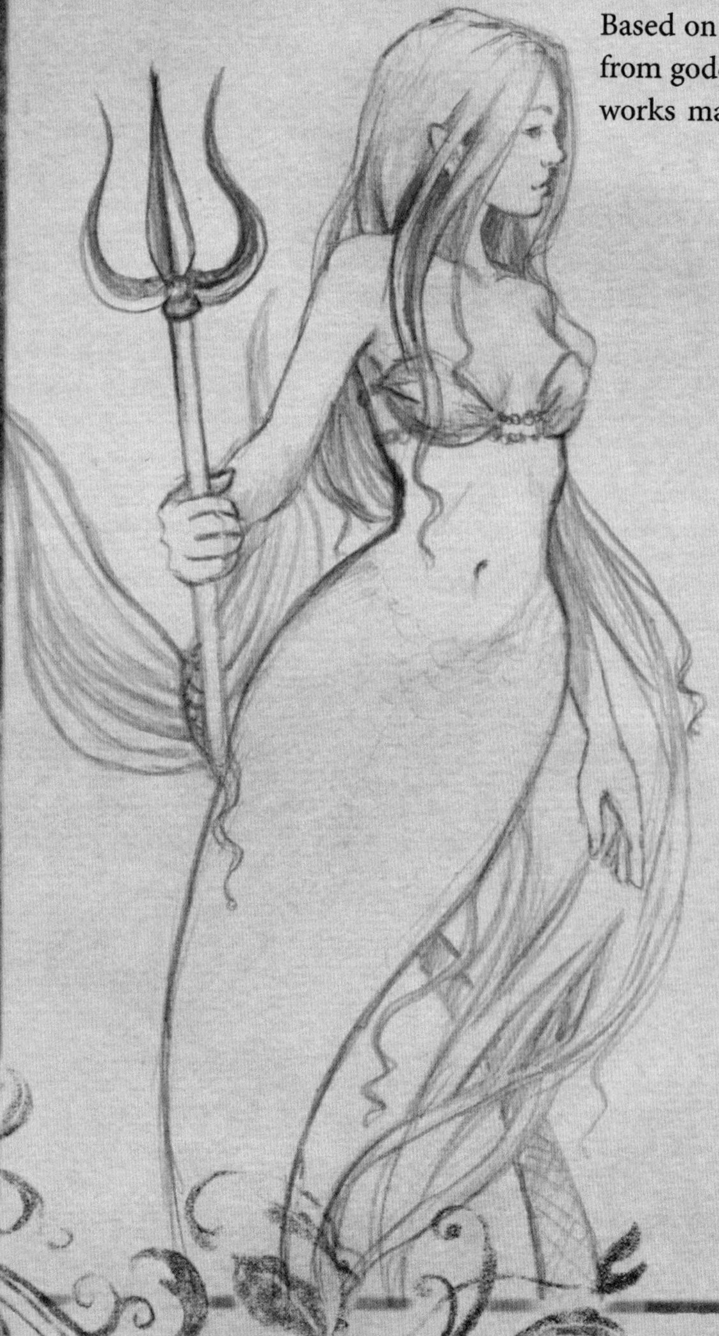

Based on an earlier artwork (Sol), this image was changed from goddess to mermaid in this recreation. This mermaid works magic with a source of warmth and power in the depths.

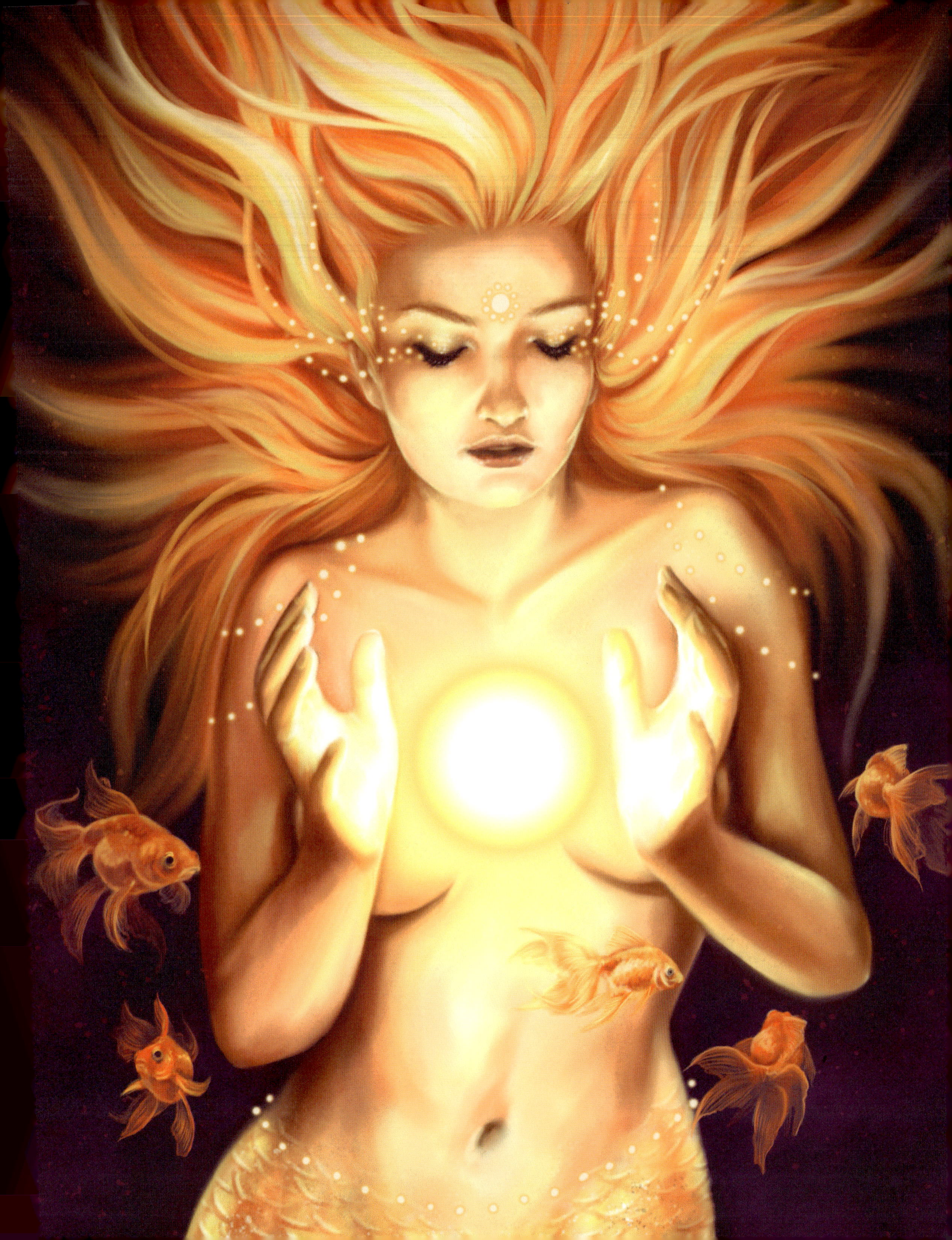

Tell Me a Secret

Digital (Photoshop and Wacom tablet), 2012

Selina imagines mermaids to be the holders of many secrets. Here, a mermaid shares a secret with another in underwater ruins. Selina used a limited colour palette and painterly techniques to create a pastel appearance with digital painting.

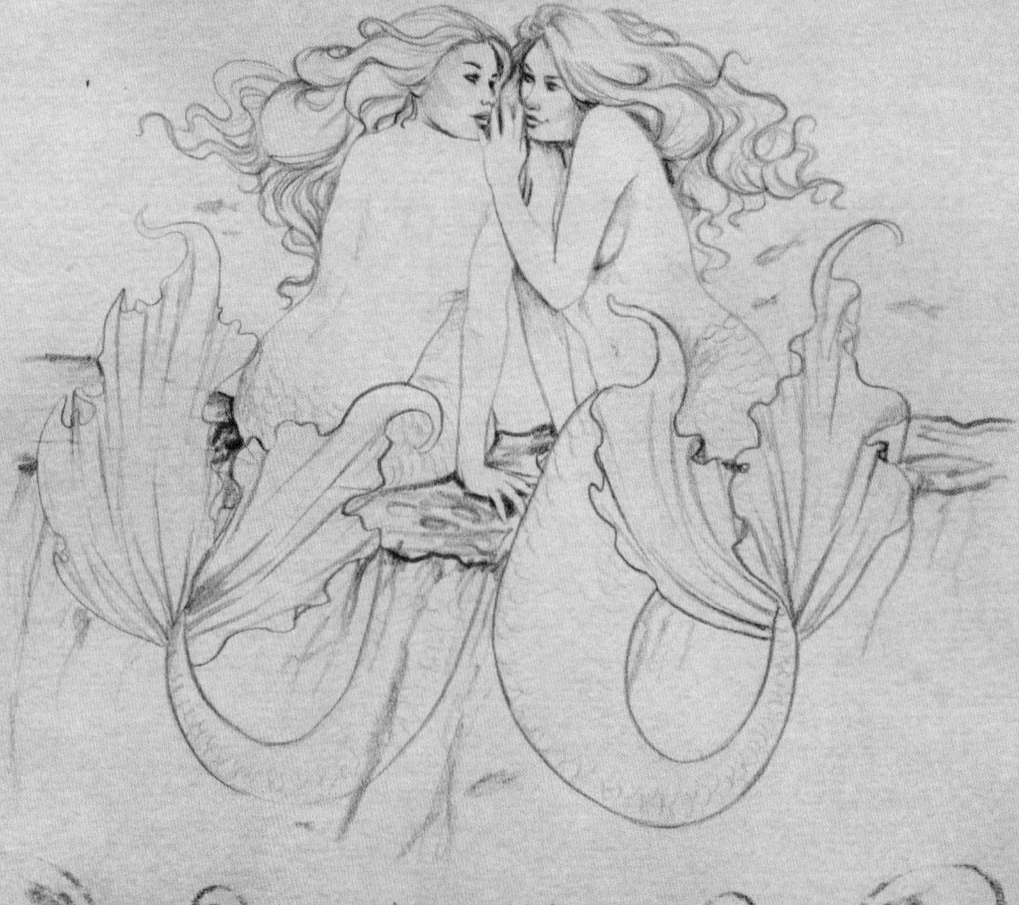

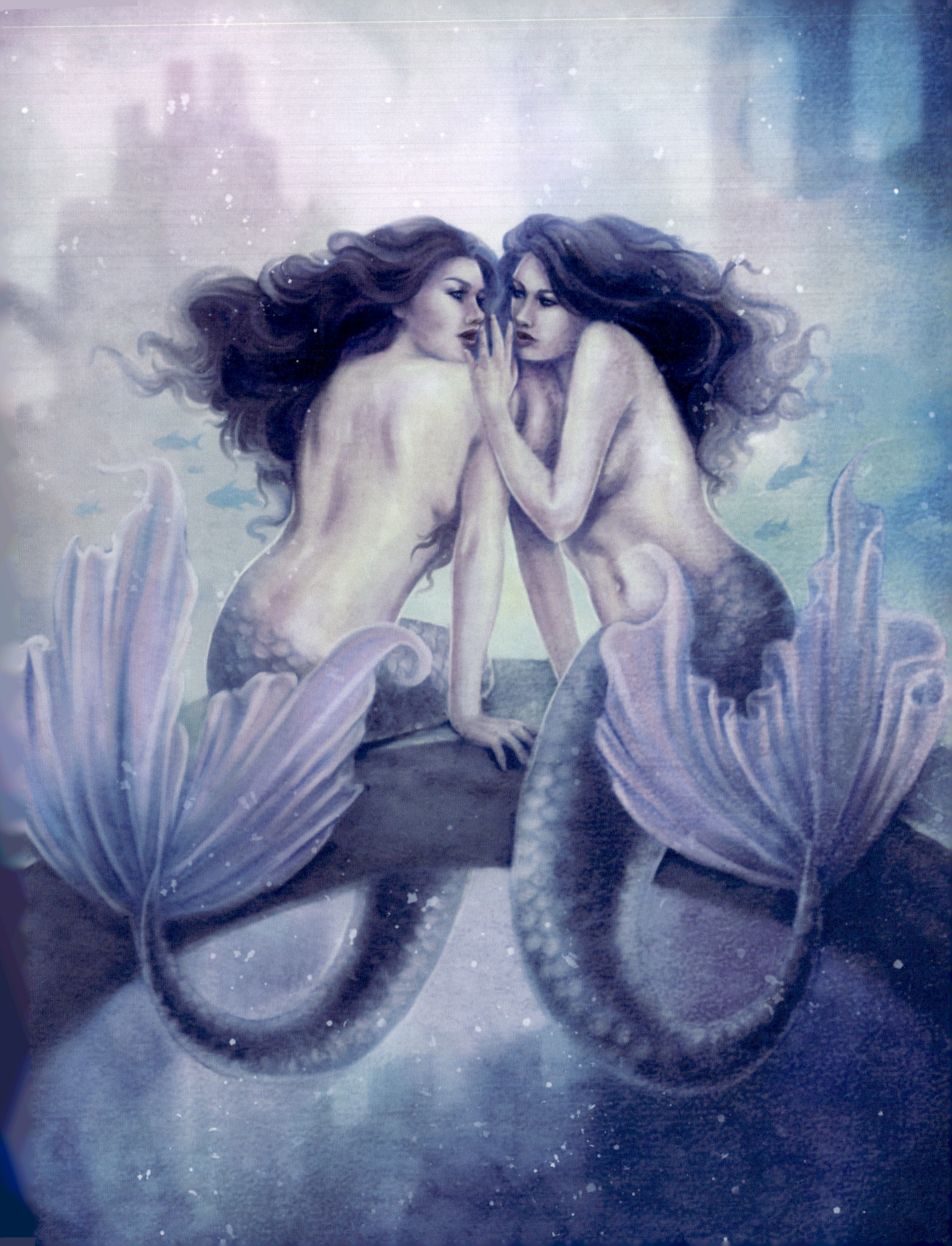

Journey

Digital (Photoshop and Wacom tablet), 2012

Selina likes to create questions in her artwork that hint at untold stories. Such as, why would a mermaid ride in a boat? Selina worked to create a pastel appearance in this digital artwork by using light colours and a limited value range.

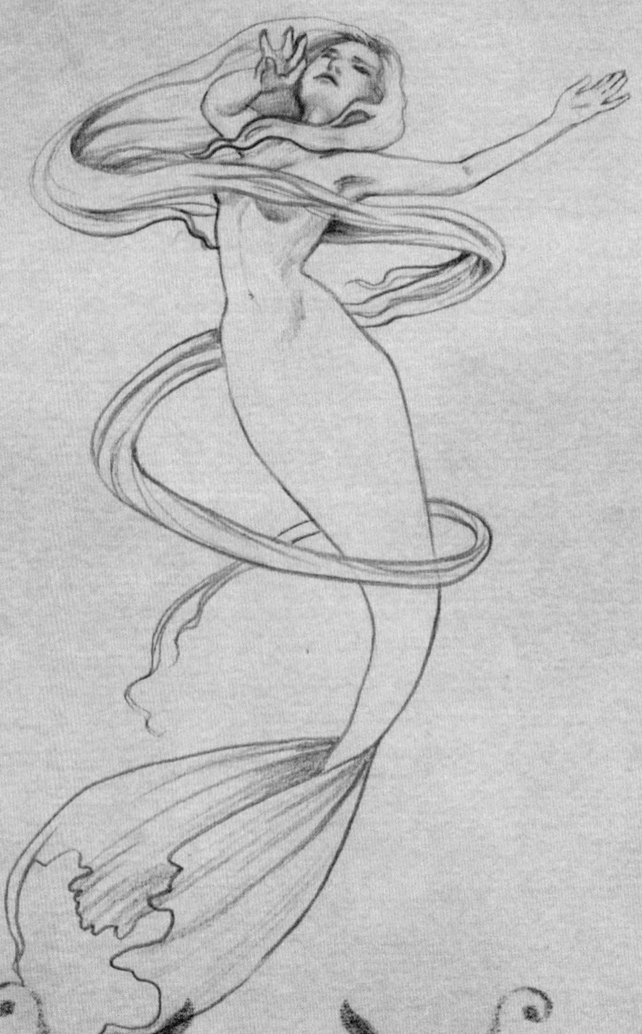

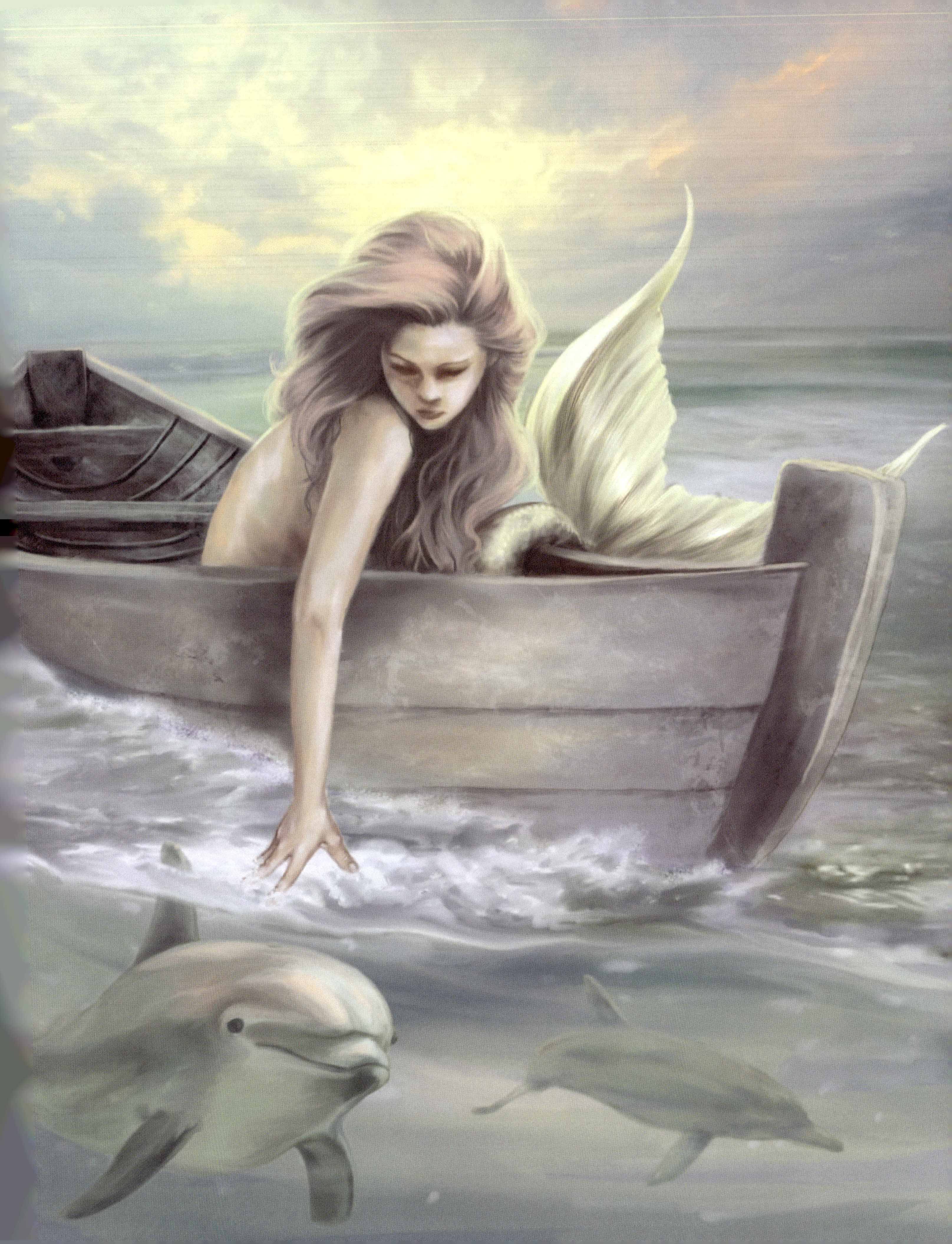

Moonborn

Digital (Photoshop and Wacom tablet), 2012

A recreation of an earlier artwork (Luna), Selina here again turned her goddess artwork into a mermaid, changing the moon into an egg holding a baby mermaid. The title of the new image, Moonborn, is an homage to the original image.

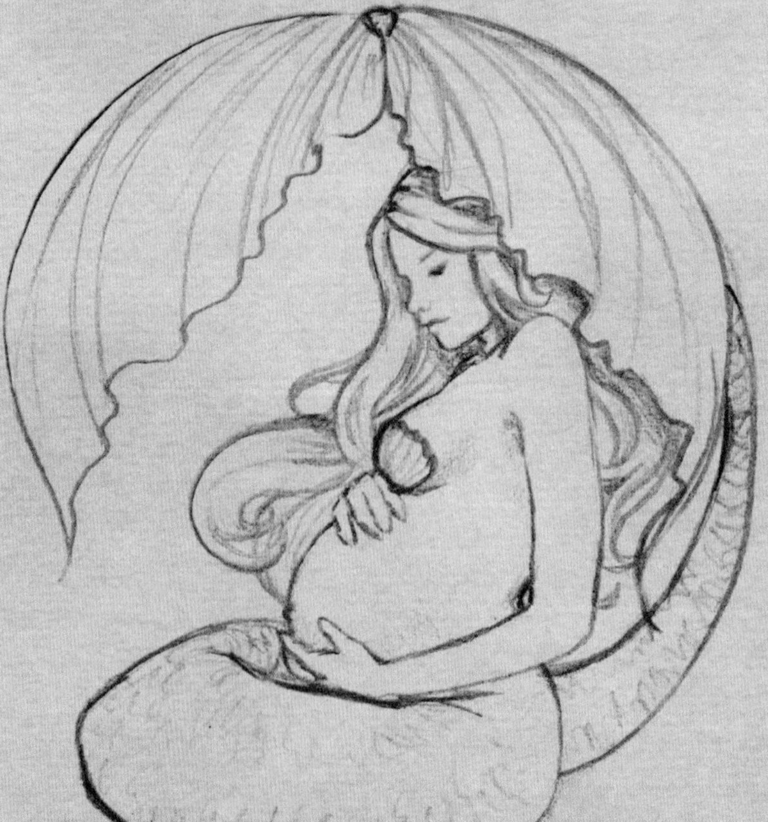

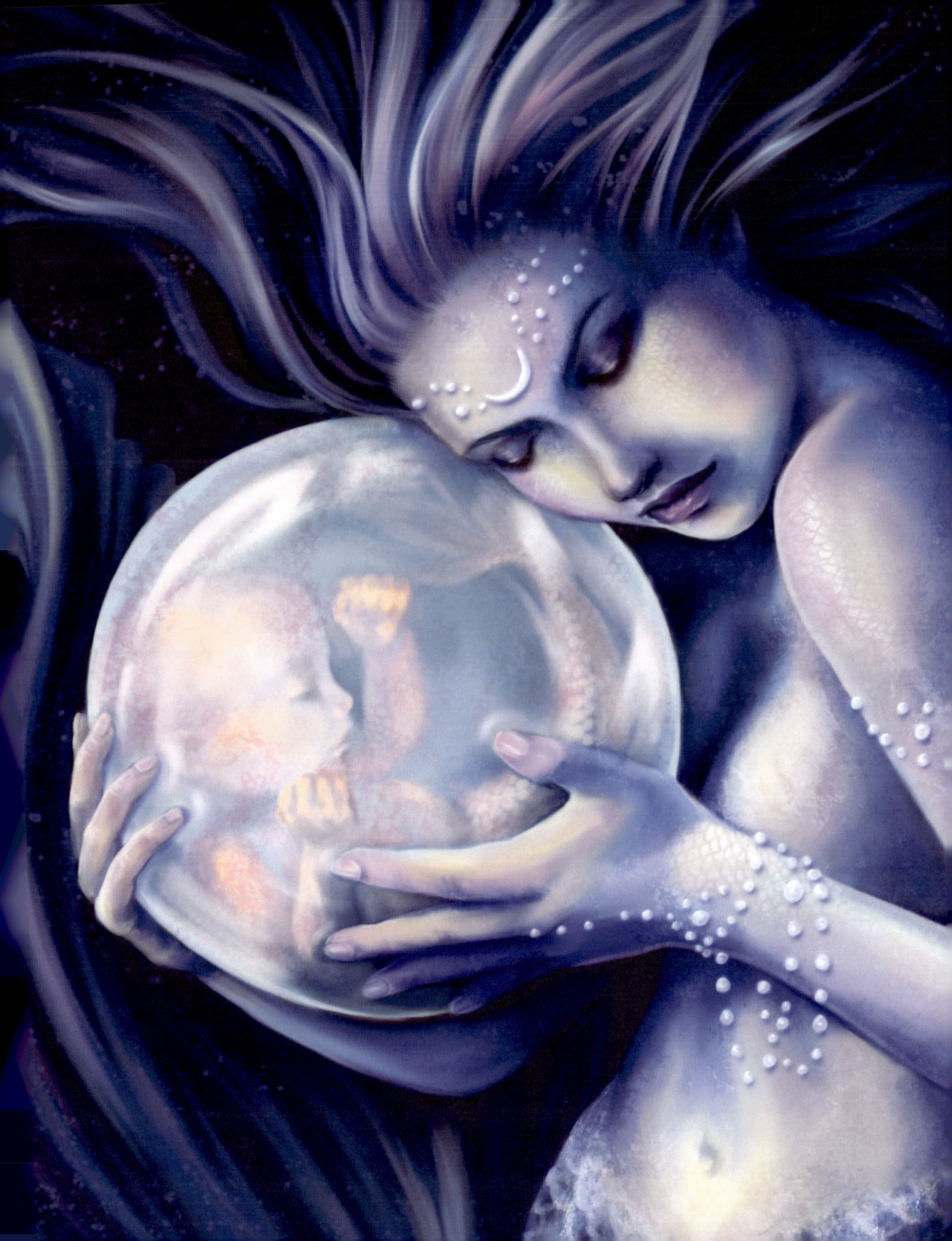

Art Collections by Selina Fenech

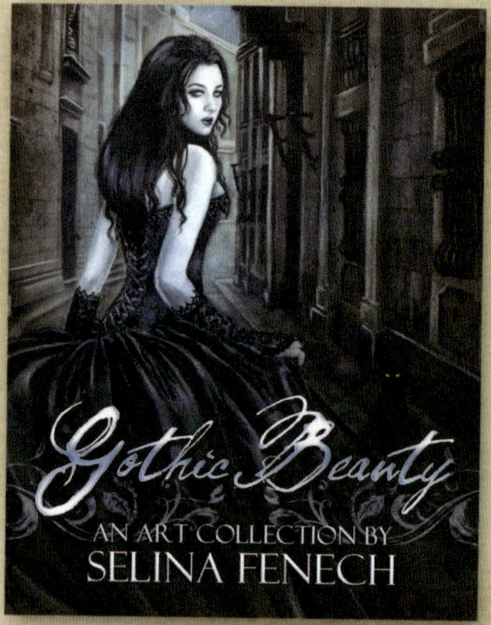

Gothic Beauty

A collection of Selina's darker artworks

Available from www.selinafenech.com and Amazon

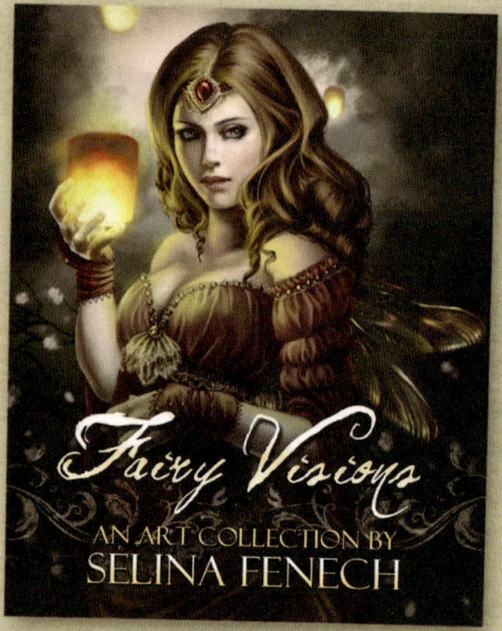

Fairy Visions

A collection of Selina's fairy artworks

Available from www.selinafenech.com and Amazon

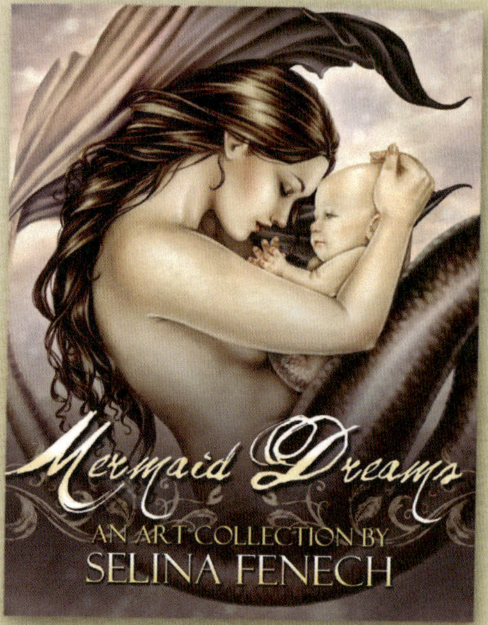

Mermaid Dreams

Selina's mermaid and water themed artworks

Available from www.selinafenech.com and Amazon

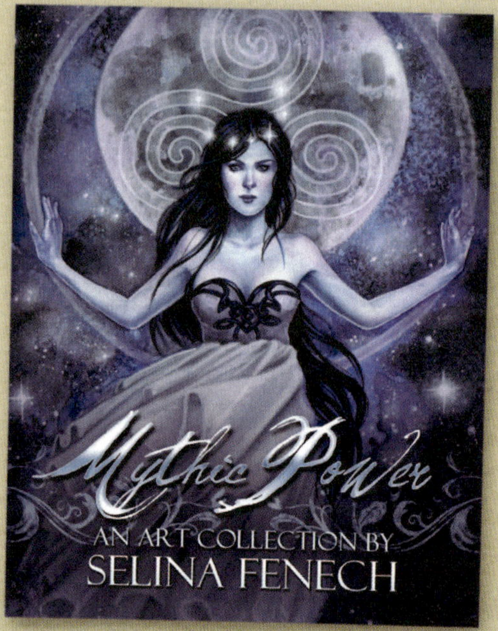

Mythic Power

A collection of Selina's mythology themed artworks

Available from www.selinafenech.com and Amazon

About Selina Fenech

Born in 1981 to Australian and Maltese parents, Selina lives in Australia with her husband, daughter, unnamed cat, and a lorikeet who's far too clever. During her life Selina has found ancient Roman treasure, survived cancer, had knights joust at her wedding, earned a living from her art, written novels and eaten every bizarre and wonderful food put in front of her.

As a child Selina loved to read. Her favourite stories were those of myth and magic, princesses and fairies. She soon learned she had a greater love than reading when she would spend countless hours staring at the illustrations in these books, ignoring the stories told in words in preference of the stories shown by the artworks. She would study each brush stroke, marvelling that any human hand could create such beauty. The images enchanted her, bewitched her, and filled her head with magic and romance. Having always enjoyed drawing, Selina began to create artworks of her own ideas of fantasy inspired by the illustrations in her fairytale books, with goddesses, fairies and enchanted creatures. She grew up continually trying to improve her art and create that same magical feel and sense of adventure she knew as a child. Many years later, Selina's artwork has been warmly received by lovers of fantasy all over the world.
Selina still resides in Australia, being self employed in painting her ideas of fantasy and selling her own artwork and handcrafted gift designs through her website www.selinafenech.com.

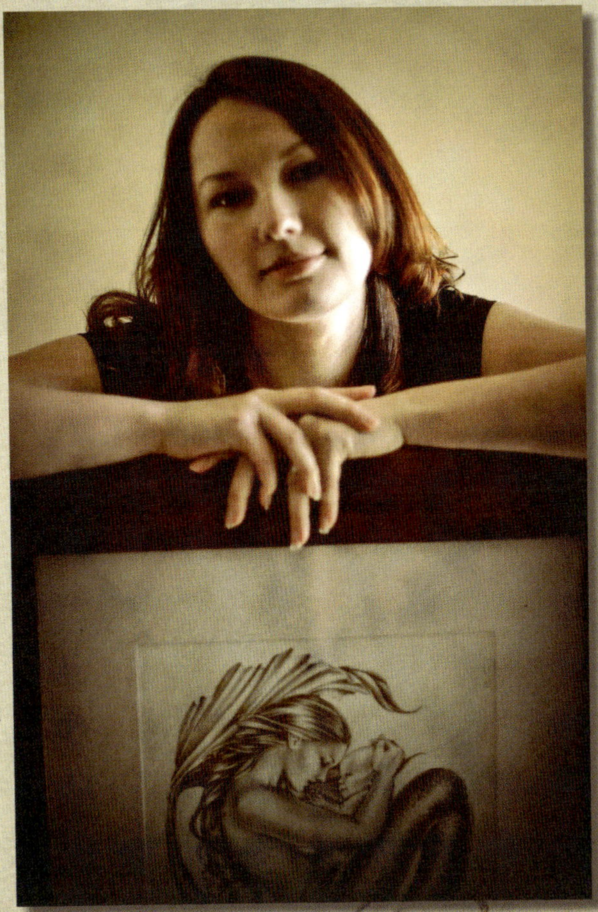

Her art has been published in books and magazines worldwide, and is available on licensed products ranging from t-shirts to stationery, figurines to jewelry. Her art has been purchased by customers and collectors in over 35 countries around the world, and she has lived off her art since she was 23 years old.

"I want to live my life like it's a fairy tale, and I want my artwork to make other people feel the same. I love that for a person of any age my fairies can bring back the magical memories and feelings of adventure from their childhood. I hope that they also create new memories and dreams of magic! As an artist, I paint because of a true, driving need to create beauty and magic. It is an inner need which I fulfill by putting brush to paper. But there is no magic there until it is shared, no joy to be found in the forms and colours until it is seen by another. So I want to thank you, for looking upon my artwork and allowing its magic to become real, for making the image I have captured in paint and pencil come to life in your eyes and mind. I hope that my artwork can be an inspiration to you.
Thank you for being a believer and lover of all that is beautiful and magical."
Selina Fenech

Other Books by Selina Fenech

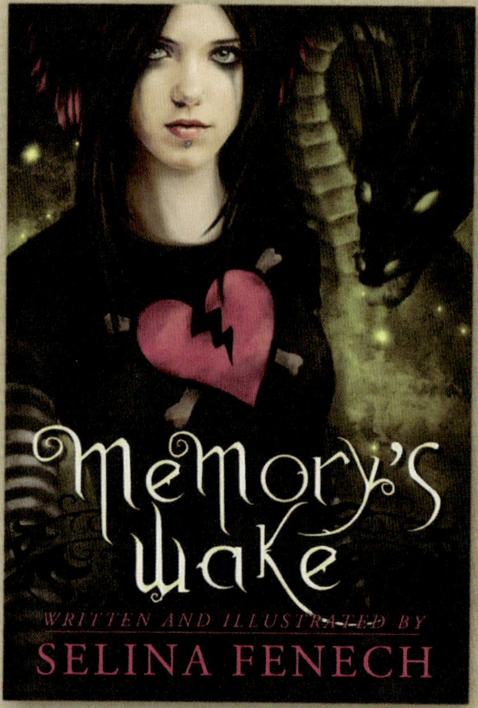

Memory's Wake

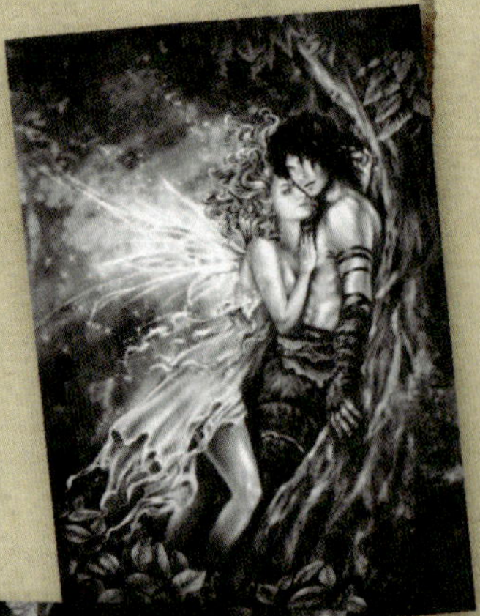

Lost in a world of magic and monstrous fairies, a troubled sixteen-year-old with no memories must find out who she is, before she is found by those who want her dead.

Memory's Wake is a fantasy novel for young adults and contains 44 black and white illustrations by the author and artist.

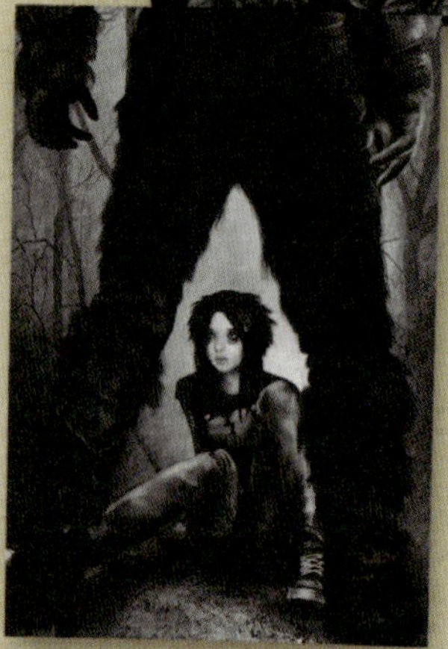

"Memory's Wake was such a beautifully written and illustrated novel that I almost have no words to express how much I enjoyed reading this book." ~ *Seeing Night Reviews*

Available As: Paperback | Hardcover | Ebook
www.memoryswake.com

Emotionally Charged

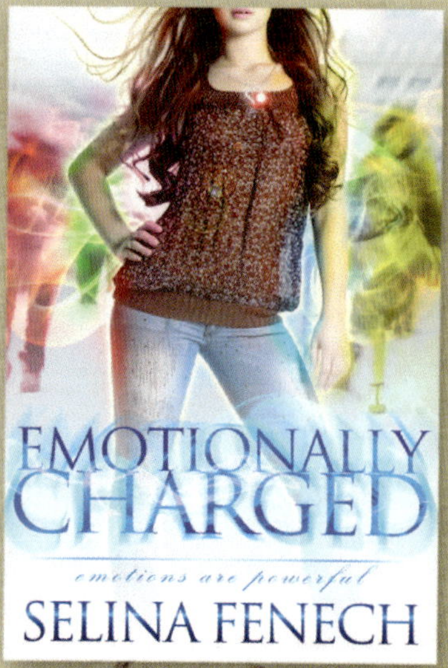

When emotions give people superpowers, what does love mean? Reading the emotions of people around her is easy for Livvy. When an earthquake strikes her city, a supernaturally attractive group of rescuers show her that her power goes beyond that. But the dream life she's been swept into seems too easy, and soon turns into a nightmare.

Emotionally charged is a paranormal romance novella for young adults.

"This was an exciting read, full of fast paced thrills, chills, and bittersweet love." ~ *YA2Bok Reviews*

Available As: Paperback | Ebook
www.selinafenech.com

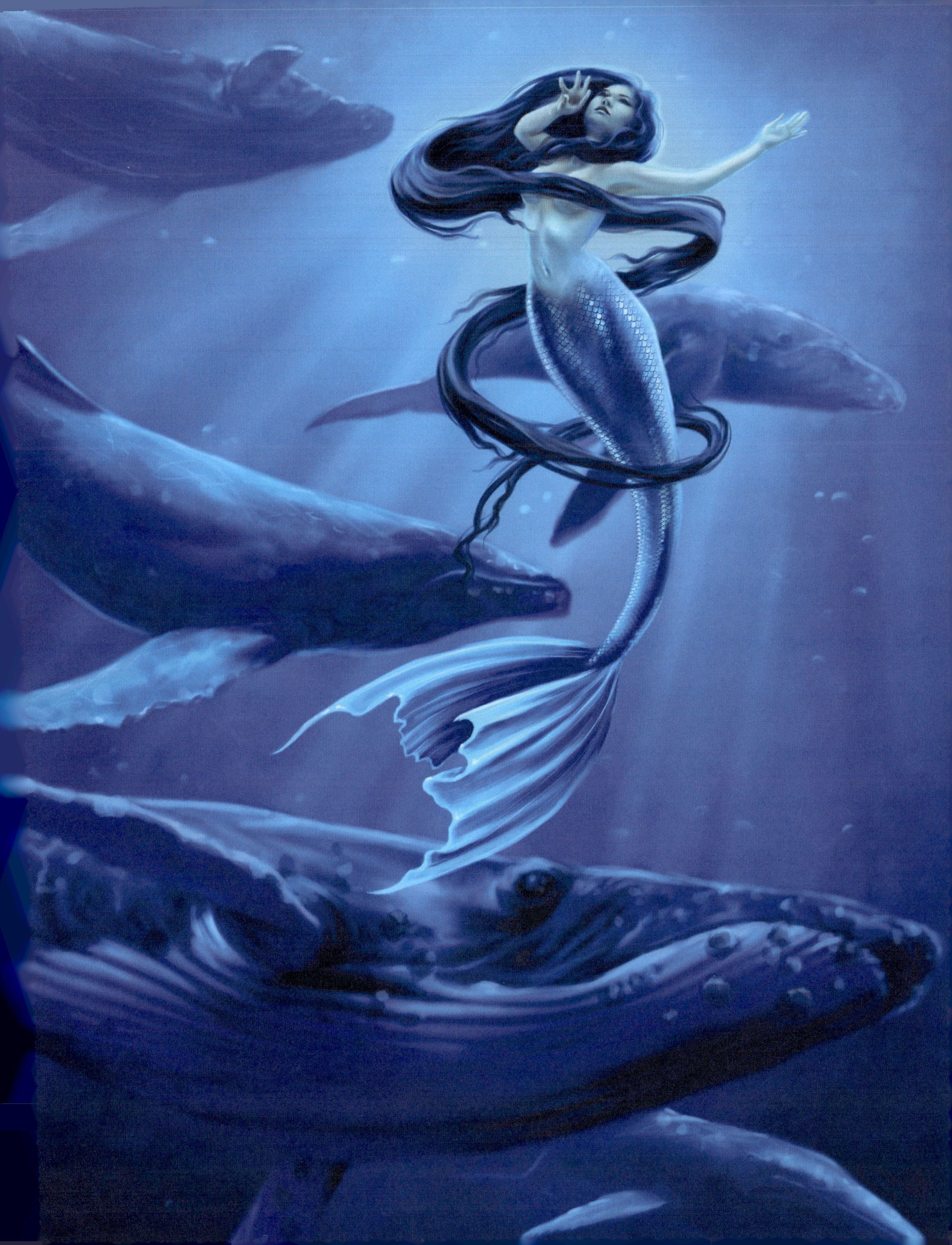

6793980R00036

Printed in Great Britain
by Amazon.co.uk, Ltd.,
Marston Gate.